The Reluctant Traveler:

How to Explore the World Without Learning Anything About Yourself or Other Cultures

by

Dan Fazio

Cover design by Mark Schwander

For Liz

Contents

Introduction (or Confession)

I hate traveling. And I hate clichés. So how's this for a double-whammy: I wrote most of this travel book while I was traveling. Ugh. Just seeing it in print is a little embarrassing. Is there anything more clichéd than a Moleskine-carrying young writer fervently scribbling down his scatterbrained ideas while sucking down cappuccinos in a bustling Roman café?

Actually, yes. Such as the dirty (but secretly wealthy) backpacker who has composed a series of poems about his amazing time in a remote Uruguayan village, where he had to subsist on grub meal for 39 consecutive days. Or the hipster chick who has returned from Botswana with a botfly living under her skin and is currently performing a one-woman show on the subject.

Have I become one of these people? Hardly.

Let me clarify. I hate travel. But I like doing awesome things. Some of the most awesome things in the world unfortunately lie outside of my hometown, so travel is a necessary evil. When I say, "I hate to travel," what I really mean is that I hate all the discomfort, confusion, fear, sickness, line-waiting and extortion that accompany the activity. Once I arrive at my destination I usually have a pretty good time.

Don't trust anyone who tells you that they actually like to travel. My wife, Liz, is one of these people. Her eyes light up at the prospect of a 20-hour bus ride, she's perfectly happy to pee in a bucket behind a Nicaraguan shack and her desire to visit any foreign land is directly proportional to the level of danger, disease and flesh-eating millipedes she can expect to encounter in said land. Still, if it weren't for her, I would have missed out on some of the greatest experiences of my life.

One final word of warning before you read any further: I am not a travel writer. Yes, I may have "written" a "book" about "travel," but you won't find long, romantic descriptions of my wanderings through the cobbled streets of some ancient village, or moody reflections upon the gothic architecture of bleak, bombed out train stations used as thinly-veiled metaphors for my mood. What you will find are true stories about cockfighting, projectile vomiting and fellow travelers pooping their pants. Proceed at your own risk.

1. WASPy Ruminations on Foreign Lands

In September of 2007, I quit my job as an advertising copywriter, sold my house, packed my things and departed on a 10-month trip around the world with my wife. Starting in Portland, Oregon, we flew to the East Coast for a week, then passed through Italy, Switzerland, Qatar, Thailand, Laos, Vietnam, Cambodia, Thailand again, LAX[1], Costa Rica, Peru, Argentina and finally Mexico on our way back to the States. We circumnavigated the globe by air, and, in my estimation, logged an additional 865,000 miles on rickety buses.

This raises a question: What the hell was I thinking? More specifically: Why would a guy who openly hates travel take on one of the most arduous travel itineraries known to man? Of course, there's a perfectly reasonable explanation: My wife made me do it.

I'm sort of joking but sort of deadly serious. Liz and I had been planning a "big trip" together for years, but in the back of my mind, I always figured we'd fly to Italy and have such a great time that she'd forget about all those damned third world destinations she longed to visit. We could snack on freshly baked focaccia and sip wine in a Mediterranean villa, perhaps taking one or two side trips around Europe when the mood struck us.

Ah, no. Liz had something entirely different in mind, and it didn't involve a lot of European self-indulgence. If she had her way, we'd be on the move every other day, camping on the edge of wind-whipped Patagonian cliffs, trekking to remote Thai villages and

---

[1] LAX is practically its own country, and a dictator-run, third-world one at that.

certainly not lounging about idly browsing the internet for hours at a time or playing video games.

We reached a compromise of sorts. We'd travel furiously for most of the 10 months, but build in several key resting points. For example, we'd start with two weeks in a Mediterranean villa. Then, after a few months of intense traveling throughout Southeast Asia, we'd get another break in Argentina, spending four weeks in Buenos Aires. Finally, we'd rest for six weeks in Oaxaca before wrapping up the trip on Mexico's Pacific coast and flying home.

Still, I was anxious (with good reason) about the whole thing. It felt like I was giving up so much. I already knew that I simply wasn't cut out to be a hardcore traveler. You know the type – wispy beard, giant backpack, claims that spooning a Nepalese Sherpa while sleeping on a one foot wide ledge at 14,000 feet was the time of his life. That's not me. Prior to our little jaunt around the globe, most of my favorite things in the world were available within ten minutes of my home in Portland, Oregon, and I'd worked extremely hard to arrange my life that way.

You know, things like cotton sheets with a respectable thread count. Good pizza. A great park and a movie theater within walking distance. Strong coffee. Stronger beer. Safe roads. Friends, family and our black lab. I wouldn't be able to enjoy any of them with any sort of consistency where we were going.

In their place I would deal with greasy synthetic sheets and tiny single beds, cockroaches, horrible pizza, Nescafe, light beer, tremendously unsafe roads, strangers, annoying young travelers and hordes of incredibly sad stray animals. To borrow a phrase from *Lethal Weapon*, I'm too old for this shit.

Of course, not all the young travelers we met were annoying. The ones we befriended often asked what we did for a living back home, and, upon learning that I was a writer, offered the inevitable follow-up question. *Oh, are you writing a book about this trip?*

I usually just smiled politely and replied in the negative, rather than sticking a finger down my throat to induce some kind of sarcastic gagging noise. I just couldn't picture myself writing a romanticized narrative about our experience. You know, the kind where the writer learns something about himself, develops a deep understanding of another culture and ultimately finds that living in a cardboard box in Bolivia is much more rewarding than his previous life in the first world. Those writers could keep their cardboard boxes; I was headed back to Portland at the end of our trip and I couldn't be happier about the prospect.

I call it the "WASPy ruminations on foreign lands" genre, and I refuse to take part. The prevailing theme of most WASPy ruminations is that although another country might be poor, dirty and overrun with locusts, it is somehow a more rewarding place to live than the author's home country (usually the United States). Actually, that's pretty much the extent of it. Replace locusts with mosquitoes, rats, spiders, poisonous tree frogs or the exotic creature of your choice, and you have the formula for the sort of travel book that will make me scoff sarcastically.

I've read a lot of books that follow this formula. A small number of them are extremely good, rather a lot more are mediocre, and every now and then one of them so enrages me that it makes me want to run the book over repeatedly with my car.

But after the 439th person asked me if I was writing about the trip, something clicked. I did have a lot to say, just not the usual dreamy travel nonsense. Therefore, my WASPy ruminations are different. I don't think that migrating from dingy hostel to dingy hostel or working as an indentured servant on an olive farm in Italy would be preferable to my current life in the United States. I may visit my share of dingy hostels, and I may pick one or two olives along the way[1], but I'll always be thinking about that plane ride back home to Portland.

So unlike some travel writers, who conveniently gloss over the massive shortcomings of living in, say, Uzbekistan, I am more than happy to point out all the dumb, annoying little idiosyncrasies of every country I visit. Rather than wax poetic about the waterfall I recently swam in, I'd rather devote a chapter to the time a Cambodian lady vomited so forcefully on the bus that it actually sprayed through the back of her seat onto another passenger's feet. Which leads us to...

---

[1] See Chapter 6.

2. Why do Asians Puke on Buses?

I fear the answer to this question may be the same as the one from that Tootsie Roll Pop commercial you remember as a kid: The world may never know. But I have a theory or two.

First, let's remove race from the equation. Asians don't puke on the bus because they're Asian – that's borderline racist and it doesn't even make sense. We met plenty of Asian-American and Asian-Canadian travelers that didn't seem to have a problem keeping the contents of their stomachs from overflowing out of their mouths and onto someone else's feet. So, it must be a cultural phenomenon – Asians puke on buses because they were born and raised in Asia, and have lived there their entire lives. With that in mind, let's explore some possible explanations.

Theory one: Most of the Asians puking on the bus are villagers that rarely ride in motorized vehicles. Therefore, they're more susceptible to car-sickness. This theory is almost completely worthless, however, as I witnessed plenty of smartly-dressed city folk quietly emptying their insides into clear plastic bags. The standard move following this procedure is to nonchalantly toss the bag out the window and perk up as if nothing had happened. Repeat as many times as necessary, or until the entire bus smells like hot noodle soup and bile.

Theory two: The bus drivers are such maniacs, and the roads are so bad, that the Asians rightfully fear for their lives and vomit in terror. There are a couple flaws with this theory as well. Flaw number one: The Cambodian lady who so athletically sprayed her section of the bus with eggy-smelling vomit did so during an unnaturally flat, straight part of the road. Flaw number two: No matter how bad the ride was, I never puked. In fact, I never saw another Westerner puke on the bus. Sure, I clenched my teeth, held my breath and prayed to gods I didn't even believe in that we wouldn't careen off the next cliff, but not once did I come close to puking.

Whatever the reason, the fact remains that Asians living in Asia puke on the bus with alarming regularity. So, smart travelers just avoid the buses, right? Sadly, it's not that simple. Not only is it nearly impossible to travel the world without spending half your time bouncing up and down in the back of a hot, crowded, smelly bus filled with ticking vomit bombs, but the alternatives aren't even necessarily that much better. I will now list the most common forms of conveyance available to the average world traveler and the specific ways in which each one sucks.

Airplanes – The Cadillac of conveyances[1], the granddaddy of getting there, airplanes seem like a pretty sweet deal on the surface. You take off your shoes and belt, get frisked, pop a Benadryl[2] and wake up in China. The downside? None, really. Unless you're Afraid to Fly. While I'm not a card-carrying, capital letter Afraid to Fly person, I do get more than my fair share of flight anxiety. And as you other anxious fliers know, every little turbulent bump can set your brain humming on a fun little fantasy about your own fiery death.

Still, when you need to get from Vientiane, Laos to Hanoi, Vietnam, and your choices are a 40-minute

---

[1] I am aware that a Cadillac itself is a conveyance. I just love using the "X is the Cadillac of Y" cliché, especially these days, when people never know if you're using it to compliment or deride Y.

[2] Okay, Xanax.

flight or a 29-hour bus ride, the flight might be a better option even if you knew in advance that the plane was going down.

Buses – We've already established that Asians living in Asia frequently vomit on buses, so, if you're in Asia, buses are a terrible way to travel. Unfortunately, if you're in Asia, they're also just about the only way to travel.

Buses are also unbelievably dangerous, especially in the third world. Think about it: The buses are old and poorly maintained, the roads are treacherous (and often steeply graded) and the drivers are usually forced to work extremely long shifts without enough time to rest. In Mexico, some rides are so dangerous that the bus company sends an employee up and down the aisles with a video camera before the bus is allowed to depart – it's so much easier to identify the remains that way.

Of course, buses do have a few things going for them. They're cheap, they depart early and often (giving you tons of flexibility), and, in some countries, they can actually be fun. In most countries, you can drink on buses. Hmm, theory number three: The vomiting Asians are actually drunk. I'll have to consider that one further.

On one first-class bus in Argentina, we were offered wine and whisky. Not wine or whisky, mind you, but both. Gratis. Of course booze barely costs more than bottled water in Argentina, but still. They also show movies on the bus. On another ride, we watched a mind-melting six movies in a row: *I Am Legend; Pirates of the Caribbean 3; The Benchwarmers; Date Movie; Bruce Almighty;* and *Liar Liar.* Yeah, *Benchwarmers* was a third-generation bootleg handicam copy in Spanish with Spanish

9

subtitles, but I think I got the gist. Of course, most buses in Asia show movies as well, but 99% of them star Jean Claude Van Damme. Minus one million points for Asia.

Trains – Trains are kind of like buses, but with a dash of added security. You can kick back and relax with the relative certainty that your engine driver isn't going to run off the rails. Additionally, people tend not to puke on trains for whatever reason, and you almost always get more personal space on a train than on a bus.

The downside to trains? *Trenitalia*. Italy's government-funded train monopoly is a shining example of why businesses that have no competition almost always fail to provide a decent product. Sure, *Trenitalia* can get you from point A to point B in reasonable comfort at a reasonable price. But you never know which *Trenitalia* you're going to get when you show up at the station. Are you going to get the train that's on time and under capacity? Or the train that's randomly 40 minutes late? Or 4 hours early? Or the train that's listed on the schedule, but doesn't actually exist? I have experienced all these varieties of *Trenitalia*, and many more.

Maybe, if you're as lucky as I was, you'll get the train that *Trenitalia* triple-booked, and you'll get to stand on one leg in between compartments mashed together with 14 other people[1] as the brakes smoke and squeal under the effort of bringing 462,000 tons of steel and human flesh to a grinding halt. In case the sarcasm isn't coming through, I'll just say that the *Trenitalia* lottery is not a fun game to lose.

---

[1] This is no exaggeration – I counted.

Boats – There are so many different kinds of boats that it's difficult to come to any kind of conclusion about them. For example, I once helped sail a yacht in the Mediterranean, from Genoa to Portofino. On a scale of one to ten, with one being a bus filled with puking Cambodian women, and ten being a Ferrari filled with supermodels, this boat ride was about a forty-six.

But then there was a boat ride from Ko Samui back to the Thai mainland that made me rethink the idea of ever setting foot on any floating conveyance again. You know the giant pirate ship ride at amusement parks? The big boat that swings violently back and forth in the air? Turns out it's pretty realistic.

Taxis – Another broad category, as there are a wide variety of taxis in the world. Not so much in the States. We have one kind of taxi, and no matter what a Midwesterner who has recently visited New York City will tell you, they are safe, they are slow, they are well-maintained mechanically and the drivers are polite. Relative to Vietnam. Ship those Midwesterners to Ho Chi Minh City and they'll see what I mean.

Oddly enough, the worst taxi driver in the world does not reside in Vietnam. He can be found in Tucuman, Argentina. The "Ethiopia" of Argentina, as it's sometimes known. The guy seemed harmless enough upon first sighting, probably because we could only see the right side of his face. Only once we had entered the cab did he turn to us and ask where we were going, allowing us to see that he had one Dizzy Gillespie-sized cheek filled with coca leaves.

Now, simply chewing a few coca leaves here and there isn't such a terrible thing. I mean, sure, they contain cocaine, but a lot of the locals in northern

Argentina do it all the time. A handful or two of leaves is said to produce a mild numbing effect and extra alertness. A handful or two. The number of leaves packed in this guy's cheek could have had Rip Van Winkle up and dancing the tango.

In any case, he took a long swig of dark liquid from an unmarked glass bottle, packed in a few more coca leaves for the road, and we were off. My knees were pressed tightly up against the dashboard in his 1978 Fiat; I wondered if they would become completely separated from my body when we crashed, or if I'd get lucky and just fly right through the windshield. I say "when" we crashed because after the first time he whizzed through an uncontrolled intersection without braking – actually, without even looking – I figured we were underdogs to make it to our hostel in one piece.

I can't describe much else from the ride because frankly I have blocked it from my memory. I do remember arriving. He overshot the address we were going for by nearly a block. No problem – he just threw the Fiat in reverse and literally mashed the pedal to the floor, casually weaving to avoid any oncoming traffic or pedestrians that didn't expect to encounter a car traveling 47 miles per hour backwards the wrong way on a one-way street.

The bill was five and a half pesos, but I gave him ten and waved off the change with a huge smile on my face, just happy to be alive. (Liz was not pleased with this... even though the difference only amounted to $1.42. See Chapter 8 for further details).

Motorcycles – I love motorcycles. At one point I tried to convince Liz that we should buy a new

Triumph and ship it to England[1]. Then we could drive through the Chunnel to France and onto Italy, Spain and other fabulous European destinations. She had other ideas, and I had no answer when pressed on how we planned on getting the bike to Southeast Asia, much less how I planned on driving it around in Bangkok without getting killed, so the plan fell through. But that's not to say we didn't ride plenty of motorcycles during this trip.

My first moto-taxi experience was actually in the Dominican Republic in 2003. I still owned my first motorcycle, a cute little Japanese inline four that I had purchased three years prior. Although I hadn't taken the official safety class, I was taught privately by an extremely competent rider, and I followed the ATGATT principle. All The Gear, All The Time, an acronym all safe motorcyclists live by.

In the Dominican Republic, a slightly-modified acronym applies. ATGATTIBGYMAT. All The Gear, All The Time, If By Gear You Mean A T-Shirt. I told Liz before the trip that I would stick by my principles and demand a helmet any time we had to ride on the back of a motorbike, but I quickly caved when I realized how silly this idea was. At least I was wearing shoes; many of the moto-taxi drivers just wore flip flops and a bathing suit.

In Asia the motorbikes are even more prevalent and ten times as dangerous. You would think that hauling your wife, your son, your baby, your dog, your groceries, five chickens and 600 pounds of industrial

---

[1] Strangely, Triumph motorcycles are far cheaper in the United States than in their country of origin, England. It's actually cheaper to buy one here and pay to have it shipped across the Atlantic than to just buy one in the country in which it was produced. Efficiency!

grade copper pipe on the back of 100cc Honda Click would be impossible. But you would be wrong.

Cirque Du Soleil-esque feats of motorcycle lading aside, the most absurd flaunting of a safety regulation I have ever witnessed was in Argentina. See, they have helmet laws there, but there's a giant loophole: You only have to *carry* a helmet with you when you ride; you don't actually have to put it on your head. So, if you're on a scooter, it's easy to just tuck the thing down by your feet. Smile and wave at the cops if you like; they are powerless to write you a ticket. Muhahahahah!

If, on the other hand, you're riding a motorcycle, you won't have room for this. Instead, you can choose from one of the following insane options:

1. Stick your clutch hand (left) through the visor opening and ride with the helmet halfway up your arm.

This looks dumb and uncomfortable, but it's nothing compared with your other choice.

2. Put the helmet on your head, but only pull it down far enough to cover your forehead.

HYaaaarghgsh!!hg11hasd;kfhlsdgas. Just thinking about how ridiculous this is makes my brain throw a rod. Have you ever held or worn a motorcycle helmet? They're really heavy! Try putting one on your head and pulling it down just so it covers your forehead. It completely, utterly sucks. It makes your head feel like a big, floppy, overgrown baby's head that hasn't developed neck muscles yet. Why on Earth would anyone ride like this? How is it not more comfortable to just pull the helmet down another 6 inches and wear it the way it's supposed to be worn?

It would be one thing if only a few riders did this. But you see them all the time in Argentina. AAAAAHdashflkasdfklsadhgsadsdsd! I have to move on before my brain gets stuck in one of those infinite loop logic traps and melts down. Keep on stickin' it to the man with your half-off motorcycle helmets, you crazy Argentine rebels. You're doing important work.

Feet – For every hour we spent languishing in planes, trains and automobiles, we spent an equal amount of time hoofing it. We walked the length of the Cinque Terre, up and down multiple Swiss Alps, the entire Byzantine maze of street vendors along Sukhumvit Road in Bangkok, you name it. In El Chaltan, Argentina, we completed a 6-hour hike to Laguna Torres and back and were later shocked to discover that we'd covered 22 kilometers.

Walking is free (though the Italians are very close to devising a way to charge for it) and provides a sort of base-level exercise that can keep you from puffing up like Jon Favreau on bowl after bowl of fifty-cent Pad Thai, but it's not without its pitfalls. Actual pitfalls. Many of the sidewalks in Southeast Asia were designed not so much to facilitate casual Sunday strolling, but rather to contain the ubiquitous above-ground sewers that would otherwise fester and ferment in the near-equatorial sun. So rather than a long strip of unbroken concrete, you get a series of loosely-fitting slabs that shimmy and totter precariously above the unimaginable filth below when pressed with the unexpected weight of a falang's[1] fat foot.

---

[1] *Falang* is the Thai word for foreigner.

Of course the sidewalks in Southeast Asia aren't the only ones in the world that make you feel as though you're playing a high-stakes game of hopscotch. In Buenos Aires, particularly the San Telmo barrio, dodging the amazingly diverse dog leavings requires near total concentration on the part of the foreign pedestrian.

All of these perils are compounded by the fact that the concept of personal space is a uniquely American idea. You can't blame Southeast Asia for being crowded; they're just running out of space. At perhaps one fifteenth the size of Argentina, Vietnam has more than twice as many inhabitants. No fooling – they have almost 90 million people in a country that's about as big as Florida (if Florida had that stomach-stapling surgery and slimmed down a bit).

So Asia gets a free pass on the crowded sidewalks issue. Not so much Italy. For a country that prides itself on being laid back and pastoral, Italy is a son of a bitch to walk around in. In the 14 weeks I've spent there over the course of three visits, the worst pedestrian traffic I've encountered was in Palermo, Sicily. Maybe the gravity is stronger down there or something, because pedestrians are drawn into near-collision after near-collision, each accompanied by a surly stare and perhaps even a muttered curse word or two.

As a generally polite and deferential American traveler[1], I usually lost this unspoken game of chicken by doing my best to make way for the locals. But my one victory, accidental though it was, was pretty sweet.

We were in Florence, having freshly disembarked from the aforementioned triple-booked *Trenitalia* ride. I was dirty, sweaty, tired and pissed that I had just spent something like 70 Euros (well over

----

[1] I know this doesn't jibe with usual stereotype. More later.

$100 US at the time) for the privilege of standing like a vertical sardine with 14 strangers for 3 hours. It was getting late, so I was making a beeline across the platform toward the bus stop in hopes we'd still be able to catch a ride to our hotel. At full speed, I looked up for a split second to try and decipher one of the confusing signs, and that's when I ran smack into an Italian guy who picked the wrong time to buzz the tourist pedestrian.

I'm much taller than the average European (6'1"), with a medium build for my height (185 pounds). And I was also carrying about 50 pounds of luggage split between my two backpacks and walking as fast as I possibly could. So you could say that the other guy took the worst of it in the collision. Or you could say that I completely fucking flattened him, which I believe more accurately describes the situation.

Now that I think about it in further detail, the collision may have been a pickpocketing attempt gone awry. The center of the platform, usually filled with hundreds of zigzagging people either trying to make a train or get the hell out of the station, had momentarily cleared. I saw my opportunity and rushed toward the exit. The moment before the collision, I was certain there was nobody around. Then the second I got distracted, some guy walked directly into my path and got demolished. I guess it could have been a genuine accident (in which case... uh... sorry, dude!), but to me it felt like glorious payback for the hundreds of times I'd been nudged, shoved, bumped, crowded and/or glared at as I was just trying to peacefully make my way down a city street.

So when I recovered my composure (as the object of greater mass in the collision, I hadn't lost much velocity and was still barreling toward the exit), I couldn't quite contain a little smile as I looked back over my shoulder. It was one of the more memorable walks of our trip. But not *the* most memorable.

No, that would be the time I walked past Ho Chi Minh's still-gleaming corpse in Hanoi, Vietnam.

3. Ho Chi Minh Would be Rolling Over In His Clear Plastic Grave If He Didn't Think It Would Freak Out the Tourists

Here's the thing: It's nearly impossible to write about Vietnam without getting into politics, at least a little bit. Here's the other thing: I'd rather have my entire body waxed and then jump into a swimming pool filled with aftershave than write about politics at any length. So, I'll just cut to the chase with the one semi-political chapter I have to offer in this book.

Ahem.

The Vietnam War seems, to me, to have been the most pointless war in the history of the world. I mean, I think war in general is pretty stupid, with very few exceptions. But this war makes the Hatfield/McCoy dispute over stolen beaver pelts and moonshine look downright intelligent.

Why? Because the Vietnamese are such great capitalists. They would deny it up and down, and they're actually insanely harsh about maintaining the appearance of a Communist state, but that doesn't change the fact that they have a nitrous-fueled free market going that would put just about anything in the States to shame.

Just walk down the street in Hanoi or Ho Chi Minh City and you'll see what I mean. Business is booming. The Vietnamese could sell ice to an Eskimo, as the saying goes, so selling bootleg DVDs and designer handbags to foreigners with fat wallets is like shooting fish in a barrel[1].

And unlike their neighbors in Laos, the Vietnamese are never bashful about soliciting business. I've seen cyclo drivers risk their very lives in a mad dash across waves of traffic on the off-chance I wanted to pay them $1.20 for a ride. When you step outside the safe cocoon of your hotel, every merchant within shouting distance is on your ass like an ill-fitting pair of counterfeit pleather hot pants.

During our first week in the country, Liz and I booked a tour of Halong Bay, a spectacular tourist destination just outside Hanoi. After busing for two and a half hours, we boarded a boat and sailed another three hours to our first stop: a remote island with a set of stairs leading to a vantage point from which to view the hundreds of limestone cliffs that pepper the bay. After oohing and aahing over the view, we climbed back down the stairs with the other tourists and got ready to board our ship for the next destination.

But then a small waterborne craft appeared out of the mist. It was a frail, elderly Vietnamese woman, rowing her ass off to reach the shore before we left. I walked down to the edge of the water to meet her when she arrived, and was bamboozled to discover a glorious array of colorful merchandise when she proudly removed the cover on her boat.

Oreos. Lay's Potato Chips. Jack Daniels. Cigarettes. Wine. Beer. This 75-pound lady was paddling an entire 7/11 around the bay all by herself. I marveled at the display, then overpaid ($6 instead of $3) for what turned out to be a spoiled bottle of wine. If there is money to be made, the Vietnamese will make

---

[1] Wow, Fazio. Two clichés in one sentence. Are you gonna justify it by saying that's how the cookie crumbles?

it. If that isn't the definition of capitalism, I sure don't know what is.

And yet, the country remains Communist, even if the Communism feels like a flimsy lace teddy bursting at the seams trying to contain the heaving, sweating bosom of the free market. Hey, they fought for their right to Communist Party, what else can you say?

But back to Ho Chi Minh. Ho, of course, was the great North Vietnamese leader who inspired his severely under-equipped side to victory against the mighty Americans. Although he died before the war was over, he became its greatest hero in Vietnam's eyes. They renamed Saigon in his honor, but that's not where his shockingly lifelike body rests today. No, his remains are on display in the north, in the city that was a virtual command center for Communist efforts during the war. Hanoi.

The name alone is so evocative. Immediately you think Hanoi Jane... the Hanoi Hilton... John McCain... Christopher Walken. That's right, Christopher Walken. Not just for his role in the Vietnam epic *The Deer Hunter*, but for the way he pronounces the word in *Pulp Fiction* when he's telling the infamous watch story to Butch. *We were in that Hanoi pit of hell over five years together.* HAN-oi. Try saying it aloud in his halting, nasally voice; it's strangely pleasurable. I've got a fever, and the only prescription is more *Hanoi*.

So. We were in Hanoi, enjoying the Pho Bo (Vietnamese noodle soup) and the Bia Hoi (fresh beer available on certain street corners for around $0.16 US), and we thought it might be a kick to go check out Ho Chi Minh's body at the mausoleum. It's free, it's easy (or so said Lonely Planet) and it's a fascinating piece of history, so why not?

Reassurances from our guide book aside, I was a little nervous about visiting the mausoleum and accompanying museum. I mean, there I was, an American for Christ's sake, walking around freely in Hanoi of all places, about to visit one of the most important Communist sites in the world. Was it really allowed? Were we sure it wasn't a trap?

Certainly any weirdness about the whole thing was on my part, not on the part of the Vietnamese. When we first arrived in the country I was similarly anxious about our shared history. Wouldn't they be pissed? The war was less than 40 years ago, still fresh in the American psyche. How would it be here, where the battles were actually staged?

Turns out the Vietnamese are *so* over Vietnam. More than us, I'd say. Anytime someone asked where I was from and I sheepishly replied, "The States," they got excited.

"America, very nice!" they said almost every time, with genuine enthusiasm. "First time here? You like Vietnamese food?"

I didn't get it. How could they be so friendly? World War II was well over half a century ago and I think a lot of Americans still don't entirely trust mustachioed Germans. And then I figured it out. The Vietnamese *won* the American War, as they call it. Back in the States, the war didn't have much of a resolution. It was getting more expensive, our casualties were mounting, there were countless protests and it was clear that our efforts were losing major points in the court of public opinion. So we gave up.

Naturally, the Vietnamese see it differently. The war didn't end with an anticlimactic fizzle in their eyes; it was a glorious triumph! They don't gloat about it, but there's a kind of proud dignity you can sense. Never mind that the average American is Donald Trump compared to the average Vietnamese; if anything, they seem to pity us more than they resent us.

"Poor guys," they must be thinking. "We embarrassed them so badly in that war and yet they're brave enough to come over here and visit. Good for them."

When we finally got around to visiting Ho, it was our second-to-last day in the city, and we were used to the mad rush of motos, the whistles and honks from the cyclo drivers and the overall cataclysm of the city's Old Quarter. So it was with some surprise that we stepped out of our cab into a whole different world.

In place of chaos, we found order. Wide, empty streets. Extremely serious looking armed guards. Special cordoned-off areas. And, most shockingly, people lining up in actual lines! We checked our bags and joined them, giddy at the novelty of not having to bully our way to the front to keep other people from cutting.

After a few minutes, it was our turn. A guard marched about 20 of us briskly to the entrance, where we were instructed by numerous signs to remain quiet, keep our hands at our sides and not chew gum or take pictures. A handful of European tourists in front of us weren't following the rules. They were loudly whispering, laughing and making all kinds of hand gestures. They may have even been chewing gum and posing for annoying self portraits with their cell phone cams (thus achieving an impressive quadfecta of forbidden activities), but I couldn't tell for sure. Just as I turned to Liz to roll my eyes at their juvenile behavior, they were silently but forcibly removed from the line, chained to a nearby tree and brutally pistol-whipped into submission by three stone-faced guards.

Just kidding. They were given a brusque verbal warning and we all marched on, through a maze of frigid gray corridors. We went up a few steps, down a few steps, turned the corner and there we were. Ho Chi Minh's final resting place.

It was smaller than I expected. The room was perhaps 30 feet by 30 feet, with a path around the outer three sides and a recessed area in the middle. Ho laid on his back behind thick plexiglass walls, cantilevered forward ever so slightly as if on some sort of eternal Craftmatic Adjustable Bed. The path was narrow, single-file, and you weren't allowed to stop moving. You could only march slowly, rubbernecking the former leader of the North Vietnamese in all his perfectly preserved glory. From the trademark goatee to the still-gleaming crown of his bald head, he was more lifelike than Amy Winehouse has ever been.

Just in case anyone got any funny ideas, there were an additional two or three guards stationed at the foot of Ho's bed, staring out into space vacantly, but surely attuned to the slightest flicker of a shutter or the red light of a verboten handicam.

A few moments later, the tour was over. We filed out into the blinding light of day, having spent maybe three minutes walking and less than 30 seconds in Ho Chi Minh's actual tomb. As we gained our bearings and tried to decide what to do next, I wondered what Ho would think of modern Vietnam. Would he decry the thousands of privately-owned small businesses and entrepreneurs that crowded the streets? Shut down international trade in favor of state-run and state-manufactured everything? Rail against the very idea of a competitive market co-existing with Communist rule? Or would he see that his people were born to compete and hopefully, eventually, thrive in a global economy?

I'm guessing he'd probably just throw his hands up and head to KFC[1] for a good old-fashioned bucket of finger-lickin' freedom.

---

[1] Franchises have been up and running in Hanoi since at least November 2006.

4. Bring Me Your Finest Meats and Cheeses

The working title for this chapter was "I'm a Big Fat American and I Like to Eat," which I eventually realized was misleading. Traveling for 10 months did make me a bit skinnyfat, but I'm hardly a poster boy for American obesity. The last four words of the working title were dead accurate, though: I love to eat, and I would appreciate it if you would bring me your finest meats and cheeses immediately.

I didn't always love to eat. I was a picky kid. My parents, bless 'em, had to deal with a pint-sized food critic, who turned up his nose at just about anything besides pizza, cold cereal and Spaghetti-O's. I grew out of it in stages, gradually developing a taste for more exotic ingredients. A little avocado, my first taste of sautéed mushrooms, and the next thing you knew I was ordering foie gras.

And now I'm picky in a different way. I have such an appreciation for the potential greatness of a food that I'm often disappointed if the real-world execution is less than ideal. I want my food made from fresh ingredients and whisked to my table at the peak of readiness. Congealed cheese and lukewarm leftovers just won't do.

Why am I telling you this? Because our trip around the world, if not entirely based on food, was at least heavily influenced by it. I mean, sure, churches and history and nature and culture are all great (I guess), but when it comes down to it, the real reason we went to Argentina was because you can get a tender, juicy steak the size of a Playstation 3 for six bucks.

So as we debated potential destinations, food always figured heavily in the equation. Italy, of course, was a given. Asia? Thai food was always a favorite, and in recent years we had both begun to appreciate a wide range of Vietnamese dishes. Argentina has the amazing steaks and wine (and the best ice cream in the world, we would later discover). But the final stop on our world tour was still up in the air.

Liz wanted to work on her fluency, so it had to be Spanish-speaking. And we wanted something relatively close to home for the final leg of our trip, so we considered the merits of places like Bolivia, Ecuador, Nicaragua, Panama and Colombia. Neither of us was exactly drooling at those prospects, especially Liz, who's still a little bitter over the time she was tricked into eating cow stomach in Quito.

And then it became so obvious. Well, obvious to me, anyway. Mexico! Yes! The magical land where tequila flows like wine and so many delicious foods and drinks begin with the letter C. Ceviche. Chorizo. Carnitas. Cochinita Pibil. Carne Asada. Churros. Cerdo. Cerveza. Chelada. And so on. Liz complained that she couldn't eat Mexican more than about once a week at home without getting stomach cramps; how was she supposed to subsist on it for three months? I brushed these concerns aside and instead focused on all the amazing beaches we'd get to visit. That did the trick. *Vamanos, amigos!*

Bags packed and tickets in hand, I was truthfully more excited for the great food we were going to eat than anything else. Screw grocery shopping and doing dishes... we were going to get to eat out for an entire year!

Early on, it was a dream come true. We ate like kings in Italy. Homemade pasta... Genovese pesto... a hearty minestrone that my great aunt makes better than anyone else in the world. And of course a long line of those fabulous cured meats and aged cheeses. If I keep going on and on about Italian food, this is going to turn into *Eat, Pray, Love II: One Man's Search for the Saltiest Prosciutto in Parma.* So let's just move on.

Bangkok started off with a bang, too. A friend who's lived in the city for nearly a decade showed us around, ordering a dazzling array of specialties we'd never heard of at every stop. And because he spoke perfect Thai, we got the real deal. No watered-down *falang* fare for us, with a tenth of the spice compared to what they serve the locals. Even without his expert guidance we found great food easy to come by. It was fresh, it was spicy, it cost less than a pack of gum.

But around the time we crossed the border into Laos, we started to crave the things we couldn't have. Things we could easily make ourselves at home. It's not that the food we were eating wasn't good – real Lao fare can be every bit as tasty as Thai, if not as well-regarded – but authentic eats became harder to come by, and the novelty of going out to eat for every meal had worn off. In Italy we hadn't bothered to cook for ourselves much because, hell, we were only going to be in Italy for five weeks – we needed to live it up. Now we were starting to realize that we'd eaten roughly 200 of our last 205 meals out, and with no way to prepare anything for ourselves in the near future, we had probably another 200 in a row yet to come.

Suddenly, I realized I wanted a pancake. A slice of focaccia. A thick, juicy ribeye. And I would have killed for a handful of crunchy tortilla chips and a bowl of pico de gallo. Knowing that the focaccia was behind us and the juicy steak and fresh tortilla chips months ahead pained me more than anything. Why did we include so many delicious destinations on our trip, only to space them out so frustratingly?

And then there was the service. Just to prepare you, I am about to complain about annoyances that may seem trivial in the grand scheme of things. Some people literally live in piles of garbage in Cambodia;

what right do I have to get snippy if our waiter ignores us for five minutes? I apologize in advance.

But seriously, the service sucks! All right, that's still a little harsh. It doesn't always suck. It's weird. It's different. It is what it is, to use a phrase I hate. And what it is, isn't American service.

It starts before you even sit down. Can you imagine any respectable stateside restaurateur trying to woo potential diners by waving a menu around outside and berating them with meaningless slogans? Even in America's most shameless tourist traps the owners have more restraint than that. Yet it appears to be standard operating procedure in every non-European country I've visited. *Hey you! You like Mexican food, good price?* And then a list. *We have enchiladas, tacos, burritos, Corona...* as if these are rare specialties that will sell me on the place. *Whoa, you guys have enchiladas? Honey, pull up a chair, we're eating here!*

The absurdity of a Mexican guy trying to persuade me to eat Mexican food while I'm in Mexico never fails to make me giggle. Of course I like Mexican food, and of course I'm going to eat Mexican food, after all... I'M IN MEXICO! But then I guess not everyone follows this logic. I am reminded of this every time I see a freshly sunburned tourist wolfing down a soggy looking bowl of Spaghetti Bolognese. We're 4,500 miles from Bologna, guys. I think there should be a rule: If you've been in the country for less than a month, you're not allowed to order any type of Italian food, including pizza[1].

Crave it, sure. Dream about it, absolutely. But don't order it. It's going to be terrible 95% of the time anyway. I mean, sure, I could have gotten Mexican food in Cambodia, just as I could have had Thai in Italy, or

---

[1] There is much more ranting and raving about pizza to come. Oh, just you wait.

Italian in the Qatar airport. But I knew I'd just be crushingly disappointed in these pale imitations of the dishes I loved, so why bother[1]?

And then there is the ironic torture of the 7,000-item menu, an Asian specialty. *Wow, look, they have every Thai dish known to man, burgers, pizza, 500 different pasta sauces, Indian and Sushi!* Yet, they would manage to be out of the single item I wanted roughly 85% of the time[2].

Whenever possible, we tried to avoid these kinds of restaurants for obvious reasons. But it's just not possible to eat every meal in some quaint local mom and pop shack. There are only so many shacks – especially in popular destinations like the Thai islands – and unless you speak and/or read the local language, it's all too easy to end up with something horrifying.

So, sometimes we'd swallow our pride and plop down at the cheesiest, most obvious tourist feeding trough in the area. As mentioned, I had an amazing knack for ordering the precise items they'd just run out of. This always provoked the same reaction from the waiters. They'd suck in their breath sharply and make a face as if I had just punched them in the stomach. *Oh sorry,* they'd say, *finish,* waving their hands like a baseball umpire for emphasis. Finish?

I knew what they meant, but I grew to truly detest this F-word, and began developing my own Pavlovian response to it. As soon as I saw that dramatic

---

[1] Another ordering rule: If you go to a restaurant that specializes in one thing, order that thing! We met a young couple in Argentina who were looking for a good place to eat. We asked if they liked steak, and they did, so we recommended a terrific steakhouse in Buenos Aires. They ordered the chicken.

[2] Probably because I stuck to the "local" dishes and refused to order any of the 4,000 Italian options or any form of burger.

look on their face, as if my order had just knocked the wind out of them and shaken their will to live, I'd fix my head at an angle and drop into a trance-like state, just staring off into space, my urge to kill rising. Very frequently, this blank stare would prompt them to suggest an alternative order. *Sir? Papaya salad finish, but we have many pasta. Maybe you like Bolognese sauce?*

The dining experience from hell, in a nutshell: Walk down tourist row, get badgered by a dozen restaurant touts, stop to check out a menu as the host intensely stares you down and/or continues to berate you, spend half an hour being ignored once you get seated, order something, get told that they don't have that thing, curse under your breath in a language the server doesn't understand, order something else, be disappointed.

All complaints and frustrations aside, in general we ate extremely well throughout our travels. We discovered new favorites, delighted in old ones and only became violently ill once[1]. But one thing we failed to do, much to my dismay, was find a single slice of truly excellent pizza anywhere outside the United States.

---

[1] See Chapter 16.

5. The Pizza Gap

Can we all just stop pretending that Italy has good pizza? Please? Just stop it. Italy has mediocre pizza at best. Sixteen years ago, when I first visited the country, they hadn't even reached mediocre yet. It was flat out awful.

Don't get me wrong; Italy does do several *pizza-like* things pretty decently. *Focaccia e formaggio[1]* is excellent. *Farinata* (another pizza-like dish made with chickpea flour) can be great as well. And if I could only eat foods from a single ethnic group for the rest of my life, you better believe I'd choose Italian. But when it comes down to actual pizza, I'm sorry, the country currently falls behind Vietnam in my global rankings.

Who am I to make such bold statements about the country that invented[2] pizza? Well, first of all, I'm Italian-American. I wish I could be proud of Italian pizza. I wish I could boast that the Italians make the best pizza in the world. Sadly, that's just not the case. America has the best pizza in the world and it's not even close. The Italians would be horrified – *horrified* – to hear these words coming out of my mouth, but like George Washington, I cannot tell a lie.

You may question my authority on the matter, but I'm here to tell you that my taste in pizza has always been rock solid. I still remember the first time I tried it. I was around seven or eight years old, at a birthday party. As the pickiest child in the universe, I didn't want anything to do with the strange "pizza"

---

[1] Literally, focaccia bread and cheese. A lot like a cheese pizza, only I've always found the focaccia to be better than whatever they usually use for their pizza crusts.

[2] Inventing something and being the best at it are not the same thing. You think Dr. James Naismith could compete in the modern NBA?

food they were serving. Finally persuaded, I took my first bite, and that was all she wrote. Pizza instantly became my favorite food in the world, and it always would be. There are very few things in life that you just *know,* but this was one of them.

Still, it would be years before I tried what I would consider to be a sublimely good pizza. And of course along the way I ate my share of Pizza Hut, Domino's, Godfather's, Papa John's, and so on and so on. Some people say that pizza is like sex – even when it's bad, it's good. I disagree. Bad pizza is garbage and should be avoided at all costs. But I can appreciate *mediocre* pizza. Chain restaurant pizza. Fast-food pizza. It has a certain comfy charm. Growing up I enjoyed a Pizza Hut pizza party like any other kid. But, despite my bad taste regarding nearly every other thing in life, I knew it wasn't the best pizza in the world. Truly bad pizza is a different story altogether. It almost makes me angry when people dare to call their wrongheaded concoction "pizza." I have no love for bad pizza. People should be ashamed.

But back to Italy. It's so tragic. Italy has all the tools to make great pizza. They make the best tomato sauce in the world. They make wonderful bread. And, of course, they invented salami and its pizza-perfect cousin, pepperoni. But in my experience the Italians generally fail to combine all these elements into a single pizza competently.

Before going any further, I have to acknowledge that despite spending a total of 14 weeks in Italy over three visits – covering nearly every major city and region from the Ligurian north all the way down to Sicily – I have not been to Napoli.

I will admit that there is a possibility that good – maybe even great – pizza exists in Napoli, given that the city is supposed to have "the best pizza in the world." If I had read *Eat, Pray, Love* before embarking on our odyssey, you bet your ass I would have gone straight to Napoli to confirm or deny Elizabeth Gilbert's claims. But, I hadn't, and I didn't, so it will just have to wait until next time. Until then, the evidence I've collected suggests that I'm not very likely to find anything better than my favorites back home in the U.S.

I'll say it again for emphasis: Americans make the best pizza in the world. And yet, American pizza has a terrible reputation abroad. Tell another traveler that American pizza is your favorite and at best they will do a spit-take and ask if you're serious. At worst they will openly mock you. *Ha, ha, American pizza? Doesn't that come with pineapple on it?*

When I was 14 and in Italy for the first time, I didn't have much tact. I also had a pretty limited palate. But I was already well on my way to becoming the world's premier pizza snob, and I hadn't found much to my liking on the visit. At one point we spent a few days with some family friends just outside Treviso. We were sitting outside chatting with Mario, the large, friendly, eerily Bono-like patriarch of the family. I was on cloud nine, having ridden my first motorbike the previous evening and fallen in love with the experience. And then we got to talking about pizza.

"So," Mario said with a big smile, reclining and putting his massive hands behind his head. "How do you like the pizza in Italy?"

I made a bit of a poop-face. "I don't like it that much," I said.

Mario's expression soured. "Oh?" he asked. "Why not?"

"Well, I can't find pepperoni," I said. "Every time I ask for pepperoni, I get some kind of weird, thick sausage. And the pizzas are really small and thin. They don't have very much cheese or sauce. And a lot of times they seem kind of dried out, or cold."

"I see," Mario said, scratching his chin. "Well, what kind of pizza do you like?"

"Oh, the pizza in America is the best. Definitely."

"American pizza?" he roared, incredulous. "With pineapple?"

I sighed and tried to explain that not all American pizza comes with pineapple and Canadian bacon. I may have reached him – opened his mind to the possibility that there is more to American pizza than Domino's and Pizza Hut and pineapple – but I can't reach everyone. There are millions that will go on loving inferior foreign pizza in ignorance and for that, I am truly sorry.

Now would probably be a good time to describe what I consider great pizza. My definition is extremely flexible in certain areas, yet rigid and authoritarian in others. First, the flexible parts. Great pizza can come in any size or shape. Big, small, personal pan size. It can be cut in traditional slices, in squares or even come as a giant uncut pie. Thick crust, thin crust, deep dish, wood-fired, New York-style, it doesn't matter, I love them all. What makes a pizza great are good ingredients in proper proportion.

Here's what I mean by good ingredients. Each component should be well-crafted and work in harmony with the other components. If you're going to make a thin-crust pizza, use a *good* thin crust, one that won't get soggy with grease and fall apart as you try to eat it. If you're going to make a thick-crust pizza, use a *good* thick crust, one with some flavor and substance to it. Not a bland, overbaked wad of dough that just takes up space in your mouth.

And the sauce. The sauce is a major weakness in most countries. First of all, they almost never use enough of it. The sauce is what makes a pizza a pizza, rather than some kind of cheese breadstick. So, ladle some on there! A thin glaze of tomato – enough to make the pizza look pretty – usually isn't enough.

Further, the sauce should have a little bit of zip to it, but not the god-awful "pizza spice" flavor that you find in most supermarkets. I won't go so far as to list exactly what ingredients should be included to make a sauce taste "right," because I think there is plenty of room for flexibility. But I'll remind everyone to follow the KISS acronym when it comes to pizza sauce: Keep it simple, stupid. You can make a great sauce from nothing more than fresh (or even canned) tomatoes, salt, pepper and olive oil. Add oregano and basil if you've got 'em. That's all you need! Make that sauce and put it on your pizza, and you're doing better than 95% of the pizza-makers in this godforsaken world. And don't let me catch you using ketchup as a pizza sauce. I'm looking at you, Cambodia.

When it comes to cheese, I have expanded my horizons somewhat. Pure whole milk mozzarella is obviously standard, but in recent years I've found that sprinkles of a second, third or even fourth variety can be acceptable. I am down with the *quattro formaggio*. In contrast to the sauce, the important thing here is simply to avoid using too much cheese. So many foreign pizzas go far too light on the sauce and far too heavy on the cheese. Don't get me wrong, I love cheese, but there should never be so much on a pizza that I'm forced to peel giant lumps off before digging in.

And finally, we come to the part of the pizza equation about which I am almost entirely inflexible: toppings. This is going to sound totally unreasonable, and I'm probably going to lose a lot of people that were with me right until this moment, but here goes: If it were up to me, the only acceptable topping on a real pizza would be pepperoni. There, I said it. Pepperoni pizza is the most perfect expression of the most perfect food the world has ever known. Enjoying the combination of flavors and textures on a well-made pepperoni pizza ranks right up there with any other experience in the culinary world. Adding extra flavors and textures in the mix just mucks things up.

I realize that this is a little out there, so I will make certain concessions to reality. I will still allow you to call your baked bread/cheese/sauce concoction a pizza if it uses any of the following toppings: pepperoni, onion, chili flakes, arugula, anchovies, green olives, black olives, sausage, Canadian bacon, pineapple, mushrooms, artichoke hearts, red peppers, garlic, spinach, prosciutto. That's it.

Unacceptable toppings include potato, barbecued chicken, peas, hard-boiled eggs, avocado, any seafood other than anchovies, whole olives with pits, slices of hot dog, carrots, broccoli, asparagus and Spam. Go ahead and make your "gourmet" feta cheese, barbecue chicken and potato trainwreck, just don't call it a pizza in my presence.

With that definition in mind, let's get back to the point: Italian pizza is just OK, American pizza is great, and very few people are willing to acknowledge these facts. But what does all of this have to do with traveling? Well, answer me this: Have you ever been to a country where you *couldn't* get pizza? Unless you've been to Afghanistan recently, probably not[1].

Can you think of a more ubiquitous food than pizza? Rice is right up there, but nothing else comes close. Every country, no matter how poor, remote and/or backward, has its own unique take on pizza. It could be as horrifying as a piece of pita bread lightly brushed with ketchup and topped with whole Oscar Mayer wieners and Cheez-Whiz, but if you call it "pizza," an army of backpackers will descend upon your

---

[1] Actually, I'd be willing to bet that you could still get pizza in Afghanistan.

establishment and wolf it down with glee. Pizza is the ultimate travel food – and often a welcome option when the local fare consists of sautéed goat rectums served on a bed of bok choy. And that's how this all relates.

I wish I could have visited every country in the world and sampled the pizza so I could provide a comprehensive reference guide for you right here. But remember, I hate traveling, and I usually hate the pizza I get while traveling, so that would be asking kind of a lot[1]. What I can offer is a general warning (avoid pizza; eat the local food), backed up with some specific examples.

Having started our trip in Italy, naturally we tried some of the pizza. We had a few decent pies, but more were soggy and over-cheesed than not. Here's how mediocre it was: I just asked Liz to choose the best pizza we had in Italy and she couldn't recall a single one that stood out. By the time we got down to Sicily we'd stopped ordering pizza on our own, but we were still forced to eat it when our relatives wanted to impress us with their local variety[2].

By the time we arrived in Asia we were ready for a change of pace. This is about the time I developed my one-month local food rule – when I witnessed untold *falang* feasting on nasty little pizzas, burgers and, of course, spaghetti Bolognese. So during our first month in Thailand, obviously I didn't have any pizza. Twenty days in Laos, no pizza. Three weeks in Vietnam... I finally broke down and tried the pizza.

---

[1] I'll do it for $10,000,000 plus expenses. Alert Bill Gates and Mark Cuban.

[2] Out of the six pies they ordered, one was edible. Most were topped with things like hard-boiled eggs, slices of hot dogs and peas in varying combinations. Thank God for that single cheese pizza.

I figured the Vietnamese would make a better pizza than the Thai or Laotian people, and I'm pretty confident I was right. There wasn't any good bread in Thailand, so you just knew the crust was going to suck. Laos has good bread thanks to the French, but I didn't get the sense that they had good cheese. Vietnam also has good bread thanks to the French, but, unlike the Laotians, they're absolute counterfeiting wizards. If they can make a fake North Face backpack that looks 100% real, why not a fake American or Italian pizza?

Putting this theory to the test, Liz and I sought out a pizza place in Hue – a town known for its culinary prowess. We ordered two pies – one pepperoni and one cheese – then sat anxiously awaiting our first taste of pizza in Asia. Lo and behold... *it wasn't half bad!* It was certainly better than any pizza we had in Italy.

Emboldened, we went on to order pizza a second time before leaving Vietnam, in a small, touristy beach town called Mui Ne. The restaurant had an Italian name, an Italian owner, and the guy who took our order was most certainly Italian as well. The pizza we received was Italian-style – small, thin-crust, light on the sauce and toppings – but it was better than any we found in Italy. We were shocked. By U.S. standards it was nothing special, but we were in Vietnam for crying out loud. Alas, success went to our heads. Well, my head. I went on to order pizza twice in Cambodia.

Once should have been enough. We were in Phnom Penh, the filthy, stinking capital of one of the saddest countries in the world. There was garbage everywhere. Rats scurrying around in broad daylight. Even things that looked pretty were most likely contaminated... like the picturesque but toxic lake that bordered our guest house.

As off-putting as the city was, we had to eat something. In a place like that, you don't mess around trying to find real, authentic food on the street. You go straight to the most touristy restaurant you can find and pay whatever they're asking for the illusion of hygiene. Sure, the kitchen could still be filled with decaying corpses, but at least we wouldn't have to see them.

You know where this is going. I ordered pizza and it was terrible. I would rank it well below the worst varieties of frozen pizza you find in supermarkets back home. And yet, I went on to give pizza in Cambodia a second chance, at a more upscale restaurant in Siem Reap. It was barely passable. Right then I decided I was done ordering pizza in Asia.

Still, I craved it. At one point I told Liz I would pay $40 for a single slice of my favorite pizza back home, and I wasn't joking. But Argentina was the next stop on our tour, and we expected to find some decent pies there. I could wait.

And now I will forgo any pretense of narrative arc and just tell you flat out that Argentinean pizza, on the whole, is the worst I've ever tried anywhere in the world. Confused? Shocked? Angry? So were we. Buenos Aires is a huge, European-style city filled with recent Italian immigrants; how can the pizza possibly be that bad?

I won't bore you with descriptions of each and every mediocre pizza we tried in the country. Rather, I'll simply tell you about the worst. We were in the La Boca neighborhood, an area particularly known for having a dense Italian population. We must be masochists because we were still subjecting ourselves to new, uniquely terrible pizzas about once a week, and there was a restaurant in the area that was supposed to have the best pizza in Buenos Aires.

We finally found the place and took a long, hard look at the menu. It was confusing, even for people with a decent command of Spanish and Italian between the two of them. Eventually we settled on a large spinach pizza with "white sauce" and a side order of faina, the Argentinean equivalent of Italian farinata. We sat down with a large pitcher of Quilmes beer to wait for our food, and I allowed myself to become cautiously optimistic.

The ensuing disaster was at least partly our fault, I'll admit. In Liz's mind, the "white sauce" would be some kind of garlic and olive oil topping. In my head, it was melted white cheese. In reality, it was béchamel sauce. In case you're not familiar, béchamel is usually an ingredient in lasagna, and is made by whisking scalded milk together with butter and flour. It has the texture and color of Cream of Wheat and, in this instance, little to no taste. In other words, it is completely inappropriate as a pizza topping.

Making matters even worse, we had forgotten that all the spinach we had previously tried in Argentina tasted like dirt. We'd tried it in salads at fancy restaurants, in grilled panini-style sandwiches, and we'd even bought our own spinach from the market and washed it vigorously, hoping to get that clean spinach taste we were used to back home. Didn't matter. *For whatever reason, spinach in Argentina tastes like dirt.* Why couldn't we remember this critical lesson when it mattered most?

The final touches on the pizza from hell: Burnt crust, no sauce (not a single dollop of tomato anywhere on the pie), no cheese and eight plump black olives (with pits) artistically placed around the outer circumference. It was weird looking when it came out, but it wasn't until that first bite that we realized it was completely inedible. I managed two bites. Liz, on the other hand, gagged her way through two entire slices just for the sake of the sweet old Italian waiter and cash register guy who helped us make our selection. It was a performance worthy of *Fear Factor*, and afterward she retreated to the bathroom and took a few pictures of her epic poop-face to commemorate the occasion.

Over the final five months of our trip I would only order pizza two more times. Discounting breakfast, that's twice out of a possible three hundred meals, or 0.6% of the time. That's a remarkable 13.7% less than my usual pizza-eating rate at home in Portland[1], but I didn't even crave it anymore. The Cream of Wheat and dirt catastrophe had completely killed my appetite for anything less than my favorite pizza back home.

A couple weeks later we were nearing the end of our time in Argentina. I'd almost forgotten about the La Boca incident, and I was looking forward to three months of tacos and salsa in Mexico. Pizza was the last thing on my mind. And then we got to talking about food with an obnoxious Argentinean girl[2] who was staying at our hostel. The topic of pizza was broached. *Ohh,* she said, her eyes lighting up when she heard that we had recently visited Italy. *Which country has the best pizza in the world? Italy... or Argentina?*

---

[1] Margin of error plus or minus 0.0001%
[2] See Chapter 9.

6. The Olive Garden

Here's a quick personality test. First, read the following excerpt from studenttraveler.com.

> *"I knew by the ring of the church bells it was time for lunch, but I was in no rush to climb down from the olive tree. The view from up there - rolling green hills splashed with red-gold autumn vineyards and the distant hilltop town of Montepulciano against the warm blue sky - was divine. I'd been picking olives in this grove since early morning. The traditional Italian harvest method, called brucatura, pulling one olive at a time off the full branches, had brought me to a state of euphoria. I'd started in the chilly early morning, my back aching from yesterday's labor in places I never knew existed, but now was warmed up, so the pain had subsided and I didn't even pay attention to the scratches on my arms or the buzz in my hands. Back home in Los Angeles, it takes hours of excruciating yoga poses to get this deep-calm-in-the-moment feeling. But here in southern Tuscany it came to me through old-fashioned farm work - by volunteering to pitch in with the olive harvest, or, as the Italians say, la raccolta[1]."*

If this sounds amazing to you, you have a personality like my wife.

---

[1] Posted by Susan Van Allen on www.studenttraveler.com, December 5, 2006.

If it sounds like a trap, hello friend, you're on the same wavelength as me.

People on my wife's side of the spectrum tend to focus on words and phrases like *rolling green hills, red-gold autumn vineyards, euphoria* and *divine.*

By contrast, people like me pick up on *chilly, early, back aching, pain, scratches* and *excruciating.*

Back when we were still planning our trip, Liz broached the idea of volunteering at an olive farm in Italy in exchange for room and board. The dollar was weaker than ever against the Euro, she argued, so this would allow us to spend more time in the country. She knew I wanted to spend as much time in Italy as possible (because I was terrified of the unknown third world countries we were yet to visit), so this was actually a pretty strong argument.

Except for one thing: I wasn't about to spend a good chunk of our trip slaving away at manual labor. I'd worked too hard to save all the money that would make our trip possible to turn around and indenture myself to some Italian farmer. And besides, what would my grandparents think? They packed up their lives and migrated from Italy to the United States in 1955, when my father was just three years old, in search of the American Dream. Now I was going to quit my job and move back to Italy to do peasant work? The news might have sent them over the edge.

Plus, I expected that the actual terms and conditions of these kinds of arrangements would fall far short of the romantic ideal that Liz had built up in her head. How many hours do you actually have to work? Do you get any days off? If so, what do you do out in the middle of nowhere on an olive farm? And what time are you expected to start working each day?

I suspect that picking olives for room and board in Italy is one of those classic travel activities that sounds good on paper but is actually quite miserable. Consequently, I'm sure there's no shortage of WASPy travelers who can't wait to sign up for months of back-breaking labor if only so they can ruminate about the experience later.

Well, not me. I put my foot down on this one. There was absolutely *no fucking way* I was going to pick olives on this trip. We had enough money, we were going to live it up in Europe and not do a lick of work for the next ten months. If olive-picking had to be a part of the experience, damn it, we'd just go to an orchard and watch other people bust their humps.

Sixty days later, I found myself squinting up into the Sicilian sun, raking plump green and purple olives down upon myself and wondering just where the hell I'd gone wrong.

I suppose the first mistake we made was budgeting so much time for Sicily in the first place. But the dollar was getting worse every day – we were burning through our money much more quickly than expected – and we knew we had a free place to stay down there. Plus we'd heard such great things about that part of the country from Liz's parents and her brother, who'd visited the previous summer. Nothing specific, mind you, just the usual post-vacation swooning. *Oh, the food*, they said. *Oh, the people.* Really, what about them?

We were considering staying with Liz's relatives for two weeks in a small town called Valguarnera

Caropepe, located in the dead center of Sicily, until Liz's brother Dave hinted through email that that might be "a bit much." So we scaled it back to 10 days, figuring we'd also take a few side trips around the island while we were there.

I started to get suspicious when nobody – not even the people in Sicily – seemed to have heard of Valguarnera. Our train tickets left off in Messina – a port city on the northeast corner of the island. From there it was up to us to make it the rest of the way. *Trenitalia* was of little help. We eventually got one of their employees to dust off a giant book filled with all the possible routes and cities in the country – in which they found that *Trenitalia* doesn't run to Valguarnera. Instead, they advised us to take a train to Catania and catch a bus from there. Ah, our first bus ride of the trip. So short and easy – we had no idea what we were in for later.

We disembarked in the center of a hot, dusty little town. Valguarnera Caropepe, at last. It was a little intimidating. Tall and pale despite both having Italian heritage, Liz and I stuck out more here than we did in the north. People in Sicily were darker, shorter and surlier looking than the mainlanders. Plus, we were carrying all our worldly belongings on our backs. I don't think the people there were used to seeing backpackers... we were like some weird pale gypsies to them. In any case, we quickly shuffled off down a side street without bothering to consult a map, anxious to escape a pack of mischievous looking teens with emo haircuts.

It wasn't long before we were completely lost. To say that the directions I'd received were sketchy would be a bit of an understatement. Rosina, the 85 year-old cousin of Liz's grandfather, had shouted them at me in roughly accented Italian over the phone. Using one hand to shield myself against the din of nearby traffic, and the other to hold the pay phone a safe six inches from my ear, I managed to remember, and later write down, a single street name: Via Taladria.

Armed with this name and my tenuous grasp of the language, we finally ducked into a tobacco shop and asked for directions. The owner had no idea what we were talking about. It wasn't just my ramshackle Italian that was confusing him; he'd never heard of Via Taladria. *Via Calabria?* he suggested. No, I was fairly certain it was Via Taladria.

Pretty soon a customer entered the store to purchase some cigarettes. This being Italy, he quickly became embroiled in the conversation and search for our relatives.

"Hmm, Via Taladria, I've never heard of it. Are you sure it's not Via Calabria?" he said. We shook our heads. At a loss, the two men gave up on street names temporarily and asked who we were looking for.

"Rosina and Calogero," we told them. Didn't ring a bell. We tried their last name. No dice. And then the magic word: Speranza. Rosina's maiden name.

"Hey, I'm a Speranza," the customer said, perking up.

Turns out the clean-cut young man who had just happened into the store was a distant relative of Rosina's. And, by proxy, my wife's. And he had a cell phone. He called Rosina, confirmed that she and her husband did in fact live on Via Calabria and offered to drive us there. If Disney is right and it's a small world after all, this town we were visiting was downright microscopic. A short ride later, we were ready to meet the grandparents.

Before continuing, let me first acknowledge that Calogero and Rosina were both extremely sweet and generous, and we are indebted to them for putting us up and feeding us for a week. That said, actually living with them is a unique kind of torture that I wouldn't wish upon anyone. And now I'm going to have a little fun at their expense, just as Calogero frequently had at mine.

Of course, none of their quirks are really that unusual, or their fault. They're just old, and they lived through a funky period in history. World War II. Mussolini. The Great Depression (which didn't only affect people in the States). That kind of shit would mess anyone up. Do you know anyone in their 80s who's not at least a little miserly and kooky? Still, Calogero is a dirty old man, and Rosina is like straight off the assembly line at the Little Old Italian Lady factory.

First, the food issues. All grandparents around the world want to fatten you up, but Italian grandparents want you to eat so much that your stomach actually bursts like that guy in *Se7en*. This wouldn't be so bad if all the food they served was edible, but most Italian grandparents in their mid to upper 80s have lost a little of their touch around the kitchen. My grandmother back home can still whip up some mean *gnocchi con pesto* and ravioli, but I can tell that it's not quite as sharp as it was when she was 10 or 15 years younger. And for every dish she does well, she will often produce a corresponding bizarre dish from the old country that has survived even after 50 years in the States.

To avoid the embarrassment and psychological torture of not being able to fully consume a particular piece of food that has been placed on my plate, I have painstakingly conditioned my grandmother to avoid offering me any creepy meat dishes or god-awful fruitcakes. It took 25 years, but now she understands that I just don't like those things, and I won't eat them under any circumstances, grandma-guilt or no grandma-guilt.

Rosina has experienced no such conditioning. She doesn't just ask if you'd like something – she makes you an offer you can't refuse. It's weird, I looked up the word *no* in the Italian dictionary, and it just means *no*. From the results I'd been getting, I thought it might mean *yes, please, keep ladling food onto my plate.*

And while the average 80-something Italian grandmother's culinary skills are sadly but inevitably eroding, so is her attention to hygiene. Dishwashers are a rarity in space-starved Italian kitchens, so it's not uncommon to be handed a plate with a few remnants of last night's dinner still clinging to the edges. The best move in this situation is to wait until both grandparents are distracted by something on the television that's blaring nearby (don't worry; there will always be a television blaring nearby), then discreetly wipe the plate with your napkin.

We were particularly disappointed in the food because we had been told that Sicily would represent the pinnacle of our culinary experience in Italy. In fact, we had it on good authority (from Liz's father, the best chef I know) that Rosina not only knew what she was doing in the kitchen, but would dazzle us with her skills. To be fair, she did a fine job on the dishes she prepared from scratch, like pasta and roasted potatoes. But then she'd turn around and serve us some lukewarm re-heated Chicken Cordon Blue from a box. Again, she's old; it's asking too much at this point to expect her to whip up something fresh at every meal, but that doesn't mean that gagging down soggy leftovers under her watchful eye isn't a horrible thing to have to endure.

And then there are the old wives tales. Aren't they one of the most perfectly-named things in the world? How else could you describe some of the crazy-ass things that old ladies believe? Old wives tales captures it perfectly.

When I was growing up, my Italian grandmother would sometimes punish me by locking me in a dark room in the basement she called the "lupo room." *Lupo* means wolf in Italian, and she once pointed to a glowing light on the furnace and told me that that was the lupo's eye, which would be watching to make sure I served out my sentence without getting into further trouble. To this day I absolutely lose my shit if a bright light surprises me in the dark.

She also had an interesting way of blending traditional grandmotherly fussing with completely off the wall superstition. When we got sick at grandma's we had to "vaporize," which meant sticking our heads under a towel above a pot of boiling water. That's sort of normal grandmother behavior, but she also used to make my father sleep with a piece of Saran Wrap on his neck when he had a cold, to "keep his neck warm." Unusual grandmother behavior. And while most grandmothers believe you can catch a cold from cold weather, ours also believed that being out in the sun during certain hours could make you sick.

As we only lived with Rosina for about a week, we didn't get to experience the full range of bizarre superstitions and rituals that she surely had on tap. But a few reared their ugly heads from time to time. For instance, she believes that sugar is great for you. She literally would not allow Liz to consume any beverage other than water that did not contain sugar, going so far as to dump heaping spoonfuls into her tea even after being told not to. When Liz caught cold, Rosina's prescription was a giant bowl of warm, heavily sugared milk. Just the thing to keep her mucus levels from reaching dangerously low levels.

If Rosina was a walking, talking stereotype, Calogero made a nice matching bookend: The dirty old man. Although his brand of mischief was completely harmless, I'd recommend vacating the premises when he gets a certain twinkle in his eye. He's what Seinfeld would call a close-talker, inching nearer and nearer until his bristly white moustache is practically brushing your cheek before starting a conversation. Then he'd speak in slow, deliberate Italian, making sure even a poor speaker like me could follow along, before building steam and turning the story into some kind of loud dirty joke that was always just beyond my comprehension. Sometimes he'd point at his crotch, or the crotch of his listener, for added effect.

Still, he remained a perfect gentleman with the ladies, perhaps talking a little too close for their comfort, but never subjecting them to the sort of things I put up with. I was whistled at, pinched, hugged, inadvertently spit upon, squeezed and – in a sequence that Liz captured on video to her endless delight – spanked by Calogero over the course of our stay.

And yet, I can deal with all those things in good humor. Bad leftovers, overly sugared drinks, a few old-man spankings – not the end of the world. No, there was something else at work in Valguarnera that made us miserable on a daily basis. Something far more sinister. I can only be talking about one thing: The bathroom from hell.

Later in our travels, we would deal with plenty of terrible bathrooms. Ones with giant spiders or cockroaches living in them. Ones without sinks. Ones without flush handles on the toilets, or worse, a filthy string lying flaccid in a pool of bacteria-laden water in place of a flush handle. Even ones that required us to walk out into the jungle in the middle of the night to use them. Out of these hundreds of awful bathrooms we'd encounter, I would rank only one[1] below the

---

[1] See chapter 16 for details on this bathroom.

torture chamber in Calogero and Rosina's otherwise fancy two-story flat.

What made their bathroom so horrible? Well, a lot of things, to be honest, but I'd have to give most of the credit to the ever-present smell of rotting diapers. Or burning human flesh. Or fermenting milk. Or whatever the hell that horrifying scent was that constantly emanated from somewhere between the bidet and the toilet.

We shared the bathroom with Calogero and Rosina, but I can't be certain whether the smell was generated by their daily ablutions or if it simply bubbled up through the plumbing. It was so bad that I always tried to break my bathroom time into 30-second increments so I could hold my breath. And yet, the bathroom appeared perfectly ordinary. Clean, even. Just from looking at it, you would never expect the foul bouquet that awaited within.

The other major flaw with Calogero and Rosina's bathroom had to do with, well, its bath. There was a tub, all right, but no shower curtain[1]. And the shower nozzle only reached my stomach. I suppose I could have taken an actual bath, but that would mean sitting in the same tub that Calogero and Rosina stewed in each morning. No thanks.

Instead I stood naked and freezing (it was around 50 degrees Fahrenheit outside and in – Calogero and Rosina never used the heat), trying to splash enough hot water up onto my torso and head to stay warm. Never mind actually getting clean – I was too preoccupied just trying to avoid the nasty smell and

---

[1] I asked Rosina why she had a shower nozzle but no shower curtain. She said that when they were remodeling the bathroom, she suggested to Calogero that they install one, but he waved off the idea as too modern. Of course he did.

keep water from splashing off my body onto the floor everywhere to give it much consideration. Afterward it was a quick sprint down the icy corridor to the only room in the house with heat, where I'd try in vain to dry off using a pack towel with all the absorbency of camel hair.

Yep, cold weather, stinky bathrooms, spankings, soggy leftovers – sounds like a European dream vacation come true! We were less than two months into our proposed year-long trip and I was already depressed. We'd blown through our budget for Italy and now we were essentially stuck spending 14 hours a day with weird Italian grandparents – not even our own weird Italian grandparents – in the middle of nowhere. Why were we doing this again?

I've tried to set the stage very carefully so you would understand what I was thinking at when the following happened: We agreed to pick olives. Honestly? After just a few days shivering in the basement at Calogero and Rosina's, it didn't sound half bad.

And now I must confess that it really wasn't half bad. Picking olives was actually kind of... dare I say... pleasant? It didn't hurt that it was one of the first sunny days we had in Sicily. And we got to take breaks to eat fresh oranges right off a nearby tree. Plus, the olives practically jumped off the branch when we raked them with our plastic tools. It was a piece of cake. Of course I should probably mention that 99% of the harvest was already complete when we started, so our total olive-picking experience was about three hours long. I'm sure I'd be singing a different tune after a full week in the orchard.

More importantly, our room and board didn't depend on picking olives; we were doing it of our own volition. As a favor to Calogero's youngest daughter, Silvana, and her husband Rino, our Sicilian saviors.

They brightened the darkest days of our trip by inviting us over for dinner, driving us to and from some of the nearby towns (anything to escape Calogero's bathroom) and offering us the opportunity to pick olives with them and their two sons. Yes, the *opportunity* to pick olives. That's how far I'd come.

As she drove us back into town from the orchard, Silvana thanked us for helping out with the olives, mentioning that otherwise they would have had to hire someone to do the job. In fact, there had been a massive argument among Calogero's children and their spouses at dinner the previous night. Some of them were in favor of hiring help during the picking season; others thought that was just being lazy. Even for a bunch of Sicilians sitting around the dinner table, the conversation got a little heated – one of the daughters actually had to take Liz and me aside and explain that everything was OK. This was just how they talked; nobody was about to get shot.

Still, the next day out in the car with Silvana, we couldn't help but laugh when she further explained the situation. Didn't she know that there were hundreds of young travelers that were willing to pick olives for room and board? The concept seemed alien to her. Why would someone – other than your blood relatives, of course – pick olives for free? I told her that it seemed crazy to me too, until I tried it for myself. Further, we told her that we would have actually paid for the experience, given how much more fun it was than rotting away in Calogero's basement, but I don't think she quite understood what we were saying. Probably for the best.

I think I learned two lessons from our experience in Sicily. The first is that picking olives isn't the worst thing in the world. Given the right weather and setting – and assuming the farmer you're working for isn't a slave driver – it can actually be fun. But take heed of my second lesson learned before rushing over to Italy and signing up: Don't do something just because it's cheap. Our time with Calogero and Rosina saved us money, to be sure, but it's safe to say it wasn't our favorite part of the trip.

Sadly, it would take more than the spankings and stinky bathrooms for this lesson to fully sink in. We kept right on doing things we would later regret solely because they were inexpensive, like booking rooms at the cheapest hostels in town.

7. Hostile Living

There comes a time in every young person's life when it seems perfectly natural to live with a crazy group of friends in an overcrowded flophouse. It can be cluttered, dirty, noisy, lawless – a borderline refugee camp – and yet everyone manages to have a great time and get along.

As intolerant of this kind of chaos as I am now, there was a time when I was at my happiest right in the middle of it. From sophomore to senior year in college, I lived with five other guys in a crumbling off-campus farmhouse that was lovingly referred to by friends, family and neighbors as "the crack house."

The exterior of the home alone was enough to warrant the nickname, as the flaking paint and moldy couches on the front porch both discouraged solicitors and set us apart from the nicer places in the neighborhood. But the dilapidated façade only hinted at the horrors within. We had a lovely patina of mold growing on our bathroom ceilings (and carpet on the bathroom floors – as you can imagine, an unfortunate choice for a house filled with six guys), a dungeon-like basement crawling with giant wolf spiders and a refrigerator that looked as if it hadn't been cleaned since the '70s.

We stole each other's food, threw darts directly into the walls, played reckless games of catch and "house golf" in every room and acquired massive collections of empty beer bottles. We borrowed hundreds of trays from the university cafeteria and used them to pave a path across our muddy lawn during the rainy season. One housemate lived out of a glorified closet and kept laundry baskets filled with clean and dirty underwear in the dining room. Another cooked up a giant batch of ramen noodles only to turn around and dump them in the middle of the kitchen floor with a flourish – an act of civil disobedience in protest of a mess that had gotten a little out of control even by our standards.

Upon visiting the crack house for the first time, one girlfriend (and later wife of one of the residents) told us that she had done some volunteering for Habitat for Humanity, and she believed we would qualify for a free house based on our living conditions. This, of course, was cause for celebration.

Honestly, we loved the place. We had our share of squabbles like anyone would, but for the most part it was ideal. But I think what happened after graduation was pretty telling. As we all found jobs and moved to varying locations around the country, every single one of us transitioned to a solitary living situation. I wasn't conscious of it at the time, but now I realize that we'd all just had enough. I got a one-bedroom apartment in Seattle and never looked back. Little did I know that nearly ten years later, at the age of 30, I'd once again find myself sharing space with kids as immature, annoying and reckless as I'd been at their age.

I should point out that not all hostels are created equal. During the course of our travels, we stayed in a few that were downright charming and peaceful. That's because there are regular hostels, and there are "party hostels." Stay away from the party hostels and you can usually at least get a decent night's sleep. Stay at a party hostel and the only sleep you'll get will be after passing out on some stained sofa following too many rounds of Presidents and Assholes.

As I said, there's a time in your life when these kinds of places are great. For me, that time has passed. I got it completely out of my system in college. But a lot of kids don't get that opportunity, instead packing their bags and heading off to foreign lands to recreate that out-of-control college experience. It's amazing how many travelers we met that seemed to live in the hostels full time. I got the sense that the whole reason they'd gone traveling was to live in a hostel and act irresponsibly.

We'd wake up in the morning and they'd be there, smoking that first cigarette of the day. We'd come back at lunch and they'd be there, cracking their first beer. Then we'd return for the evening, worn out from doing whatever kind of tourist stuff we'd been doing, ready for bed, and they'd be in full-on party mode – reggae cranked and ready to rock.

Flush with diligently-saved cash at the start of our trip, we didn't think we'd need to stay in many hostels over the coming year. But Italy was far more expensive than I remembered. The last time I visited, in the year 2000, they were still using lira, and the exchange rate was around 2,400 lire to the dollar. When Italy adopted the Euro, they decided across the board that just under 2,000 lire would equal one Euro. Fast forward to 2007, and the Euro was kicking the dollar's ass. To put our purchasing power in Y2K terms, we were now getting just under 1,300 lire per dollar. In other words, everything was about twice as expensive as I remembered.

Plus, we hadn't exactly been frugal. Not counting home-cooked meals or dinners hosted by friends and family, we were dropping an average of $30 every time we fed ourselves. Add a week in Switzerland – one of the most expensive countries in the world – and by the time we reached Rome we were already on the hunt for cheap hostel dorm beds.

The first one we found fit the bill perfectly. We could get two beds in an eight-bed coed dorm for 11 Euro each. Easy call. We trudged up four flights of stairs with all our gear (the elevator was out of service, naturally), located our room and burst through the door exhausted from a day of traveling, ready to collapse onto our beds for a long, peaceful night of sleep.

Instead we found a loud, booze-fueled card game in progress. About eight young travelers were perched around a small desk at the far end of the room, listening to Euro dance music on someone's laptop and whooping and hollering as each new card was turned over. Cue the needle being yanked off the record player. They took one look at us and knew we weren't in the mood to party.

To their credit, the other travelers didn't seem too hacked off that we'd just crashed their game. They were friendly, and even moved the card game to another room down the hall without us having to ask. They could have kept playing in our room for all I cared; I just wanted them to get off my bed so I could pass out.

We ended up staying four nights, booking only a single night at a time even though we could have gotten a small discount by committing to a four-night stay up front. See, we intended to move each day. *I've had enough of this shit*, I thought to myself as I tossed and turned through the night, trying to ignore the thumping music and random drunken hollering down the hall. But every morning we found our resolution had faded at the prospect of actually getting all our stuff together and lugging it to another hostel that would be more expensive and only slightly less terrible.

What made the place so bad? Let's consult the crappy hostel checklist together and find out.

Does your hostel have any of the following? Check all that apply.

- Crowded, filthy, barely-functional bathrooms?

- Packs of nihilistic, chain-smoking European backpackers?
- Rude, disinterested staff?
- Tiny beds?
- Dirty beds?
- Creaky beds?
- Cockroaches, bedbugs, giant spiders and/or rats?
- Horrifyingly unsanitary kitchen facilities?
- Mysterious smells?
- Loud music playing at all times?

Our place in Rome rated a six out of ten – far from ideal, to be sure, but not among the worst we'd encounter during the course of our travels. And after four nights there we were flying to Southeast Asia, where, Liz promised, we could find perfectly acceptable non-hostel lodging for under $10 a night[1]. We wouldn't stay in another hostel for months. And though we'd end up dealing with some fairly miserable conditions in Asia, at least we always had a private room to retreat to. Even if that room did happen to be infested with rats.

When we finally moved on to Argentina and Mexico, we said goodbye to guest houses and hello to a whole new set of European style shared-living hostels. Aside from our time in Buenos Aires and Oaxaca – and not counting actual hotels – we wound up staying in 19 different hostels. And because we were actively trying to save money by this point, we started using their kitchens.

---

[1] Her claim proved to be true, but I always argued that we shouldn't settle for "acceptable" at $10 when we could have "luxurious" for $20. I did not frequently win this argument.

Around this time I started to get pretty nostalgic for my old crack house kitchen. The large collection of mismatched dishes and silverware... the congealed pasta sauce on the stove... the unidentifiable furry things in the fridge... it was all coming back to me. These disgusting hostel kitchens were just like the one I'd used throughout college.

Just as quickly, I remembered how miserable it was trying to actually cook anything decent in the crack house. Back then I hardly ever attempted to prepare complicated dishes because I simply didn't care. Boil water, add pasta, add store-bought sauce. Repeat 5,000 times or until you graduate, whichever comes first.

Nowadays my tastes are a little more refined. Even though the grocery stores in Argentina weren't very good, I'd still dream up elaborate dinner menus and do my best to track down the right ingredients. Then I'd find myself jockeying for position on the stove for the rest of the night with 15 kids that were trying to boil water for their ramen.

The few places that actually had decent kitchens were almost worse than the ones that were flat-out horrible, because they tempted us into thinking we could cook like we did back home. If we walked in and saw a dead rat sitting in a saucepan on the stove, no problem, we'd just go out to eat. But if we saw miles of available counter space, sharp-looking knives and eight gas burners, well, that was occasion to get our chef on.

Unfortunately everyone else seemed to think the same way. One hostel we visited in El Bolson, Argentina, had a glorious kitchen. Consequently, everybody that stayed there cooked in, every single night. While I was ambitiously trying to bake bread from scratch and whip up some pan-fried white beans with pancetta and sage, I kept bumping into two French guys working on a complicated Beef

Bourguignon and a German guy making a hearty stew out of about 500 ingredients.

Another place we stayed in Mexico appeared to have a pretty decent kitchen on first glance. It was outdoors, covered with a tarp, and it had a massive, professional-looking short-order grill right there for anyone to use. At check-in they fitted us with bracelets that we would have to present to be admitted to the kitchen area the following morning. Apparently locals sometimes tried to sneak in to partake of what the owners described as a "really great" breakfast.

The next morning, we headed to the kitchen area, flashed our bracelets and prepared to be dazzled by a breakfast so good it had to be protected with an extra level of security. Boy, were we disappointed. It was a "cook-your-own" breakfast, and nobody had told us. They provided a few ingredients – eggs, white bread, pancake mix and a handful of spices and seasonings – but nothing else. If we had known we'd be cooking ourselves we would have picked up a few extra things at the store.

Burnt out on eggs and toast, we opted for the pancakes. Bisquick or not, American-style pancakes actually sounded pretty good. I whipped up the batter and waited my turn for a shot at the grill. As I was in the middle of flipping my cakes, some vaguely European guy sidled up to the grill next to me with his own batch of batter. *Those are really thick for pancakes, no?* he said, eyeing my food skeptically. Actually I thought I had made them pretty thin by my standards, but I just shrugged. He shrugged back at me and proceeded to dump his watery pancake solution all over the place without so much as greasing the grill. Later, when I saw him walking around with the pale scraps he'd managed to scrape onto his plate, he was still muttering about how awful the pancakes were.

I got news for you buddy. What you call pancakes, we call crepes. And if you were trying to make crepes out of watered-down Bisquick using a grill that was barely warm enough to brown a piece of bread, well, let's just say that I don't think you should be the one giving me tips on how to cook.

The next day we got the bright idea of using the eggs and white bread to make French toast. There was a little bit of cinnamon on hand[1], and we'd seen someone else do it, so we gave it a shot. Liz threw together the batter and I manned the grill, sharing space and spatulas with at least three other people. Since I didn't have sole possession of the grill, and it was taking forever anyway, I casually wandered around while our sad little pieces of toast sputtered away.

I came back just in time to find a disoriented-looking young backpacker wandering around the grill area with an empty plate. He looked like he'd had a few the night before – or maybe a few that morning – as he puttered around aimlessly wearing a blank expression and one of those hilarious multicolored tank tops that only the Danish and Swedish seem to wear.

He muttered something in the general direction of another group of people that were using the grill, and, without getting a reply, casually picked up a spatula and stole a piece of French toast right from under my nose. I didn't even say anything... I was just in shock. I mean, nipping a pour of someone else's milk for your coffee is one thing, but actually walking up and taking food off the grill while they're standing right there? Ballsy.

But I was becoming numb to the casual rudeness one encounters while traveling. I was so used to people cutting in line that I didn't even try and stop

---

[1] But no vanilla. Hello? We're in Mexico, people! There should be vanilla.

them anymore. You want to light up a cigarette right next to me while I'm chopping vegetables? Go for it.

The same numbness was creeping into our discretion when it came to choosing hostels. We'd file off the bus in a zombie-like state, strap on our fifty pound bags and usually end up taking the first room we looked at – simply because we didn't want to walk any further.

The situation came to a head in Tilcara, Argentina, when we wound up staying in a place with a giant stain on the wall right above the bed. Was it blood? Urine? Semen? All of the above? We couldn't say for sure. The disturbing thing was that we had agreed to take the room without fully comprehending how disgusting it was until later.

The incident prompted us to make a rule. From then on, we were obligated to check out a minimum of four hostels before making a decision. No matter if it was 100 degrees outside and we'd just come off a 20 hour bus ride – we'd pound the pavement until we found something acceptable. We stuck to this rule hard and fast... for approximately five days. Then it was right back to the cheapest, easiest and usually crappiest hostels near the bus station.

Let this be a lesson: Traveling for 10 months is hard. When you've reached the point where you'd rather sleep under a mystery stain in a room with smashed mosquitoes all over the walls than lug your bag around for a few more minutes in search of a better place, you've been on the road too long. Or, it could be that you're simply too cheap.

8. Budget Traveling – For the Love of God, Don't Do It

Are you rich? Think carefully before answering. If you're reading this book, the answer is "probably," even if you're on a break from the night shift washing dishes at Denny's. The fact is that even poor Americans are ridiculously wealthy relative to most of the people in the world. And that holds true even as the U.S. dollar looks more and more like toilet paper every day.

A lot of travelers feel guilty about being rich, or at least say they do. Sometimes they volunteer or donate money as a result, and that's nice. Personally, I don't feel guilty. I feel extremely lucky. I was born into an upper-middle class white family in the United States toward the end of the 20th century. Do you know how insanely fortunate that makes me, historically speaking? Very few people have ever had it as good as I do. That's not to say I haven't worked hard to achieve success, but if life is like a video game, then I'm playing on a 50-inch plasma with all the cheat codes in hand, while people in, say, Cambodia are doing their best with a broken controller and a cracked 1970s Zenith with no sound.

Most other travelers are in the same boat. After all, traveling just for the sake of traveling is a luxury, and an expensive one at that. We met locals in Southeast Asia that hadn't so much as visited the next town over, and couldn't comprehend why anyone would leave their hometown for any reason other than work. I began to realize that most of the people we met – even the ones that worked in the tourism industry – didn't really have an appreciation for how wealthy the average traveler was.

It actually started to make me nervous. Although we found Asia to be remarkably safe – more so than most parts of Europe, actually – if the guy driving our tuk-tuk[1] realized that we had enough money to feed his family for the next 100 years, what's to stop him from kidnapping us? Thankfully, I don't think they know just how good we've got it.

For me, the sheer absurdity of the wealth disparity between us and the locals was particularly striking. Why? For a few years leading up to our trip, I worked a second job to save money. And by "worked a second job," I actually mean "gambled professionally," obviously.

In fact, roughly 100% of the money we spent during our 10 months abroad came directly out of my poker winnings. We would never have been able to manage 10 months without any income if it weren't for my degenerate gambling ways. I usually avoid telling people about this because there are only two possible outcomes. Either they don't believe me, or they are fascinated and want to talk about poker nonstop from that point on.

Truthfully, poker is boring. Having studied and played about 15 hours a week for the past six years, I find I can hardly stay focused on the action anymore unless I'm playing for a lot more money than I should be. Take my word for it: Being a professional poker player sounds way more glamorous than it actually is. Anyone with a basic grasp of probability and math can become a winner in the game if they keep their emotions under control and stick to stakes they can afford.

But poker, boring as it is, does have one bizarre side effect: If you're good at it, you become numb to the real value of money. For the truly great players, money has no value whatsoever; it's just the measuring stick they use to determine who's winning the game. That's

---

[1] Essentially a motorbike rickshaw taxi.

why you hear about the top players doing things that sound absolutely ludicrous to the average person – like wagering $100,000 on a game of golf, or ordering a $1,000 shot of booze at a Vegas club. Money is worthless to them, and that's precisely why they are able to win so much of it.

See, you have to attain this sort of Zen attitude about money to become successful at cards, because you will often lose, and lose badly, even when you play perfectly. The key is making the best possible decisions over the long term. An opponent can play terribly and still take all your money in a single hand when their long-shot draw comes in. You have to be able to take that loss in stride and throw another wad of cash on the table, because deep down you know that if he keeps playing that way, you'll get your money back and then some.

This has always been the hardest part of the game for me, and probably explains why I've only ever been a modest winner. I accumulated my small poker fortune as one accumulates pennies in a jar: tediously. It's just the way I am – a saver, not a spender.

Even so, poker has distorted my perception of money tremendously. I have bet hundreds of dollars with what I knew to be the worst hand – an outright bluff – and won. I have won $650 on a single hand of poker. I have lost more than $1,000 in a day on multiple occasions in a single month and still come out ahead. One time, when I was having trouble with my game, a fellow player advised me to actually light real $20 bills on fire to help drill a healthy disrespect for money into my head[1]. Suddenly I found myself in Asia, trying to talk a tuk-tuk driver down from $1.50 to $1.25 for a ride. Huh?

---

[1] I did not follow this particular piece of advice, but honestly, it probably would have helped me become better at poker.

It was really hard for me to adjust. After all, haggling is an integral part of traveling, and you often find yourself dickering over a sum hardly worth picking up off the sidewalk. Some people will actually get mad at you for not haggling. I overheard other travelers complaining that newbie tourists make the prices higher for everyone by just paying whatever the vendor asks. I guess that's probably true, but how can it possibly be worth five minutes of my time to save 75 cents? I could play cards for half an hour, lose $100, and not bat an eye. So why can't I just pay the extra 75 cents for the convenience of not haggling?

Of course Liz was a real stickler about haggling, and damn good at it to boot. But something about it felt hypocritical to me. On the one hand, she's a generous tipper – especially in third world countries where it's appropriate. And she has volunteered her time and money in several extremely poor countries. But at the same time, she will gladly haggle with a Bangkok street vendor down to the last miserable baht over a purse that costs less than $5 US. I didn't get it. Why did the people working in restaurants deserve her money more than the guys camped out on Khao San road?

Of course the street vendors are definitely out to screw tourists and will happily sell you something at a much higher price than they would a local... but even their vastly marked up goods are still cheap by our standards. If we really felt so bad about these people being poor, shouldn't we just pay whatever they're asking? They wouldn't stay poor for long.

Now obviously there is a difference between donating time or money to a worthy cause in a third world country and simply overpaying for the things you buy on the street. But if you were truly concerned about a country's economic well being and development, wouldn't you do both? The street vendors and tuk-tuk drivers need money to feed their families just as much as various causes need supporting.

The truth that a lot of travelers don't want to admit is they *need* countries like Thailand and Mexico to remain relatively poor. If Thailand were rich, it'd be just like Hawaii – stunningly beautiful, but too expensive and developed for your average broke hippie to visit. As it is, just about anyone in the States with enough money for plane tickets can hop on over to Asia and live like a god. How is that fair?

Don't worry, I'm not going communist on you here. I'm pretty sure that a certain degree of economic disparity is a necessary thing in the world. And while a capitalist, profit-driven society certainly has its share of inherent flaws, I'll gladly take it over the alternative. Which I'm pretty sure involves listening to a suitcase-sized transistor radio for news about the latest purges while you wait in a bread line.

Neither am I saying we should stop volunteering or donating money to people in need. I just think we need to be honest about it. Help out your favorite causes, and don't stress out too much if the counterfeit Bathing Ape T-shirt you want to buy costs $6 instead of $5.

Now I need to address my wife directly so she doesn't divorce me over this chapter. Liz: I don't think you're a hypocrite. In fact, I think you're one of the most generous, giving people on the planet. You're a social worker, for crying out loud. But the next time we're in Tucuman, Argentina, and I tip the cabbie an extra buck-fifty, I would appreciate it if you didn't flip out. I'm just supporting the economy. And now we're even!

9. America the Hated

When you're attempting something as complex and daunting as traveling for 10 months straight, there's absolutely no way to remain in control all of the variables. This is especially true concerning the timing of your adventure. Sure, you can pick a departure date, but with some destinations three, six or even nine months away, a lot can happen before you arrive. You know, flooding, hurricanes, riots, a complete economic collapse – and I'm just talking about traveling within the United States. Insert drum zing here.

Fortunately for us, the timing of our round-the-world adventure was mostly good. We planned on renting out our house while we were gone, but ended up selling it at the perfect time instead[1]. We swung by the Burmese border well before the massive flooding that turned the entire region into a quagmire. And we were particularly lucky in Argentina – we left Buenos Aires just before a series of protests that clogged up the streets near the bus station and limited the transportation of beef into the city (the horror!) and we managed to make our way through Patagonia before the Chaiten volcano erupted, spraying the normally photogenic surrounding landscape (which we had just photographed) with ash.

Not everything worked out as well. We were in Europe during a period of historic lows for the US Dollar relative to the Euro. We arrived in Oaxaca City just before the anniversary of the 2006 riots, and another major protest was scheduled to go off right on

---

[1] One friend likes to say that ours was the "last overpriced house sold in Portland," before the real estate bubble burst.

our street[1]. And, worst of all, we found ourselves traveling during a period in which Americans had the worst international reputation that Americans have ever had, ever. Ever[2]!

There was a time when, at worst, traveling Americans were regarded as well-meaning but lowbrow bumpkins. More often, we were idolized as wealthy pop culture gods, blitzing our way through foreign lands aboard a figurative gold-plated hovercraft, spewing a bounty of American dollars, Levi's Jeans and Coca Cola in our wake.

We are no longer as well-liked. As fellow Portland author Chuck Thompson puts it in one of the few travel books I thoroughly enjoy (*Smile When You're Lying*), Americans are the new Germans. Seemingly every other country on the map has some sort of beef with us. And while most of the people we encountered throughout our travels were perfectly friendly to us as individuals, almost everyone had some harsh words for the old US of A[3].

I'm still hoping to skirt the issue of politics here as much as possible, but I think even most Republicans would agree that a lot of this was George W. Bush's fault. Yeah, his approval rating wasn't so hot even in his own country, but overseas, people really seemed to think he was Hitler. As Americans traveling in foreign lands, we absorbed more hate for W than a couple of communist vegans might absorb at a monster truck rally.

---

[1] The 2008 event was peaceful and we were able to watch the march from our window.

[2] Post-election update: The world seems to like us again now that we've elected Barack Obama.

[3] Again, the only country in which we weren't berated at least once or twice for being American was Vietnam. Which is, of course, insane, considering how recently our country bombed their country.

An Italian policeman. An Australian father and son. A Mexican single mother. A Canadian surfer. And of course, my favorite snotty Argentinean hostel worker.[1] These are just a random sampling of the hundreds of foreigners that accosted us with anti-Bush, anti-American rhetoric with arguments that ranged from somewhat plausible (Bush is a puppet; the war in Iraq was based on false information) to borderline retarded (Bush is Hitler; 911 was perpetrated by the US government).

Look, I didn't much care for Bush or many of his policies, but I still think America is a great country. Yeah, we've done some terrible things, but what country hasn't? Measure our atrocities against all the great deeds we've done and I think we come out looking pretty good. I guess what I'm saying is that I'm hardly a flag-waving patriot, but it still gets my hackles up when people make completely ignorant statements about my country.

Cue the Argentinean girl (AG from here on out). We were on the Andean side of Argentina, in a small town called El Bolson. It's probably the closest thing South America has to Eugene, Oregon – a self-proclaimed "nuclear-free" city in a spectacular natural setting that is consequently filled with all manner of nouveau hippies. Liz and I had settled into one of the cooler hostels we found anywhere on our trip – a giant house tucked away into the woods on the outskirts of town, in the shadow of a majestic mountain range. We befriended a British woman traveling by herself and spent the next few days hiking and mountain biking in the surrounding wilderness with her.

On one excursion into the nearby town, the three of us ran into another group from our hostel (including the AG) and got to talking about accents.

---

[1] The same girl I referenced in Chapter 5.

See, the British gal was from Yorkshire and had an accent that sounded Scottish (like Desmond from *Lost*) to me. Questioned about our own accents, we explained that we didn't really have any in the Pacific Northwest – we pretty much speak like the people on the news. And then I made the mistake of asking the AG whether she liked British or American accents better.

Hold on, hold on. It's not as dumb a question as it seems. When I traveled to Europe in 2000, I met plenty of people that absolutely swooned over my American accent, even though I sound as plain as the guy explaining how to work your seatbelt in a flight safety video. I know that this sounds like the premise for a Bud Light commercial, but at one point I was approached by an entire Italian women's volleyball team just so they could hear me speak English. Accents are funny – I mean, Paula Deen sounds absolutely ridiculous to me, but I'm sure she'd cringe if she ever heard me speak. Foreigners especially seem to prefer a good Southern twang or an East Coast snarl to my boring non-accent.

But that was then and this is now, and now people kind of hate America. So I guess I shouldn't have been surprised by the AG's reply. *Oh, I hate American accents.* The forcefulness of her answer was a bit of a shock, considering that her English, while heavily encumbered by an Argentine accent, was far more American than British in both vocabulary and pronunciation. *But of course you do realize that you're speaking with an American accent right now?* I asked her.

She was horrified by this. *I would never speak in an American accent!* she said... in an American accent. I turned to our British friend for support, but she gave me a knowing look that said, "Look pal, I realize that this girl sounds about as British as John Wayne, but I'm staying out of this one."

I shrugged and was ready to let it go, but then the AG felt the need to lecture me about a number of vague American transgressions against Argentina. Now, I'm no historian, but I was pretty sure that *England* and Argentina had gotten into it war-style over the Falkland Islands less than thirty years ago. Still, I kept my mouth shut and let her say her piece.

A few minutes later, the conversation having drifted on to safer subjects, we all decided to get some ice cream. But just as we were about to head over to the shop, the AG disappeared. *Where did she go?* I asked our British friend. She rolled her eyes. *[The AG] went to exchange some of her money.* Huh? Weren't we in Argentina? Wasn't she Argentinean? What kind of money did she have?

It turns out that, in addition to speaking with an American accent despite hating America, this wonderfully misguided Argentinean angel also *kept all of her money in American dollars!* You can't make this up. See, a lot of Argentineans don't trust their own currency or their own banks. The Argentine Peso collapsed in 2001 when, spooked by the country's massive debts and ridiculous unemployment rates, citizens began withdrawing them and exchanging them for dollars, then sending the money abroad. This run on the banks led to further collapse and devaluation of the peso and helps explain why you can still get a $30 steak for $7 in Buenos Aires.

Perhaps I shouldn't be too smug about all this, considering that the US appears to be heading down the same road and, until recently, I had my life's savings stashed in a Washington Mutual bank. Ahem. In any case, every time the AG received a paycheck, she went and converted the pesos into dollars, then presumably stashed them under her mattress or in a coffee can. When she needed to spend money, she would take some of the dollars and convert them to pesos on a case-by-case basis. According to our British friend, this helped the AG save money, because it was a pain in the ass to do a currency exchange every time you wanted to buy something. And, like many other Argentineans, she simply didn't trust the bank.

At least this poor, confused girl's hatred for America was based on something semi-real. I couldn't make heads or tails of her various conspiracy theories, but they were political in nature, and given our run from 2000 to 2008 I can hardly blame her for chastising our politics. What I *can* blame people for is chastising American tourists for being loud, arrogant, culturally ignorant boors. The truth is, we are almost never any of those things.

I know this goes against the current stereotype, but I'm here to tell you that the current stereotype is dead wrong. Think about it. People in other countries basically assume that everyone in the USA is like Cousin Eddie from *Christmas Vacation,* and to be fair, some of us live up to that image. But would Cousin Eddie really spend his vacation mucking around in a third world country? Hell no, he'd go somewhere easy – to an all-inclusive tropical resort where the staff speak English and wait on him hand and foot.

Meanwhile, the kind of Americans that travel in Asia, Africa, South America, the less popular European countries – hell, anywhere but the world's hugest, easiest, safest tourist vortexes – can't get enough of the local culture and, if anything, tend to be *too* respectful and polite. These are people like my wife, who value all cultural traditions equally, even if they involve cannibalism or throwing babies off of cliffs. *Oh, your genital mutilation ritual is so charming and authentic!*

RELATED STORY: Near the end of our travels, Liz and I found ourselves in an extremely remote Mexican fishing village known only to an elite group of world-traveling surfers. By elite, I don't mean that they were elite surfers. I mean these people were living the surf lifestyle at a world-class level – the most slack, nonchalant, blissfully lazy group of people I have ever encountered. Imagine the cast of *Dazed and Confused* starring in *Point Break* minus the bank robbing[1].

Anyway, this little surf paradise is a peninsula, but it might as well be an island, as there isn't anything resembling a real road connecting it to the mainland. You have to take a boat, which means the place is extremely well isolated from most of the rest of Mexico. There really isn't much to do other than surf, drink and play cards, and neither Liz nor I can surf. Naturally, it wasn't long before we fell into the hypnotizing uber-slack lifestyle that permeates the place, renting a crumbling shack and accompanying hammock on the beach from a charming local family, then sitting back and doing absolutely nothing for about a week.

One day we returned from some particularly spirited nothing – that may have actually involved bathing[2] – to find our host family all dressed up. Anything other than a ratty T-shirt and bare feet meant it was a very special occasion, and they informed us that some independent filmmakers would be screening a movie about their village that night – projected onto the wall down at the abandoned basketball court nearby. Some of the family members were actually in the movie, and they invited us to come along and watch it with them.

So, of course we quickly got "dressed up"[3] and followed them through a back-alley maze down to the court. As we approached, we fell into line with streams of other people, locals and traveling surfers alike, pouring from every possible pathway before excitedly

---

[1] As far as I know.
[2] A rare activity in those parts.
[3] Put on shirts.

converging into one mass exodus toward the first real "activity" the village must have seen in ages.

The excitement down at the court was palpable. The entire village was there – if the Ex-Presidents needed to rob the village's single sad little convenience store to further their surf adventures, this would have been the time for it. But they must not have needed the cash, because they were all milling around with us, waiting to watch an exciting independent film.

Cue the movie. It was in Spanish, of course, and nearly unintelligible due to the sounds of many of the village's children, dogs and chickens running and screaming throughout the show, but it became clear rather quickly that it was the heartwarming true story of one man's quest to bring the venerable Mexican sport of cockfighting home to his little village.

No fooling. All the semiotic cues were there... the cloying footage of children playing, the interviews with beaming friends and family, the gorgeous atmospheric shots of local scenery with just the right hopeful, evocative music bed – this was a feel-good story about a local hero. And then we came to the part where he affixed the razorblades to the mighty talons of his prized fighting rooster. I'm happy to report that Liz and most of the surfers were properly horrified.

But back to the main narrative thread. Despite our patience for and/or appreciation of many questionable foreign customs and practices, somehow the reputation of the traveling American as shouting, littering, culture-destroying mass consumer has spread worldwide, even though, as I hypothesized, those kinds of Americans don't tend to get too far away from America. As a result, the majority of Americans abroad (who *are* respectful travelers) have to put up with snide little comments and thinly-veiled criticisms from all sorts of other travelers wherever we go. Even though the very people berating us often turn out to be *just like the stereotypical Americans they're criticizing!*

It is unfuckingbelievable that Americans are widely considered rude when 85% of the rest of the world can't figure out how to line up in a proper line. It's crazy that we're considered the loud ones when it is fairly standard for Australians to hold a shouting, beer-chugging and pushup contest any time more than three of them convene in one spot. And it's mind-blowing that everyone thinks we're the ones taking over the world, when Israelis always seem to travel in groups of at least 38 and often completely dominate entire hostels, restaurants and bars.

Of course, the totally unjustified hate runs both ways. While I think our reputation as poor travelers is way off the mark, I concede that Americans, on the whole, are extremely xenophobic at home. These days we seem to have just as much beef with the rest of the world as they have with us. Take France, for example. First world country, old world pedigree, rich in history, member of the European Union, thoroughly decent modern society by any metric. Not a bad resume. And yet if you held a foreign country popularity contest among the red states, I'm guessing France would narrowly edge Afghanistan and Iraq for third-to-last place.

Obviously most of the US hate for France is misplaced, but there is something very French about pissing people off, so you can kind of see where it comes from. It's like on *The Simpsons,* when evil mastermind Hank Scorpio builds a giant death ray and asks Homer which is his least favorite country – Italy or France. Homer shrugs and says *France,* to which Scorpio laughingly replies, *Nobody ever says Italy!*

Full disclosure: I've been to France three times. I studied French in high school. I enjoy French fries, French bread, French kisses, French toast and French wine. I like stinky French cheeses. I like French cuisine. Hell, the French pretty much invented "cooking" as we know it. My father's family is from a part of Italy that is *very close to France*. Okay, I don't like French dressing, French manicures or French poodles. I am indifferent to the actor French Stewart. And I wouldn't go so far as to call myself a Francophile. But I'm certainly more sympathetic to the country and its people than the average American.

Now, a lot of Americans dislike the French because of the whole Iraq War thing. France surrenders. Ha, ha, what pussies. And yeah, they kind of crapped the bed during World War II. But dig a little deeper and you'll find that the French were actually pretty bad-assed throughout history. They popularized public beheadings. They had a war that lasted a hundred years. A hundred years[1]! And under Napoleon, they controlled huge portions of Europe and even tried invading Russia. If you still want to hate the French, by all means, hate them; just don't do it because you think they aren't tough enough.

In fact, I'll give you a valid reason for hating France: Parisians are dicks. They live in one of the most amazing cities in the world, and yet they walk around with their noses in the air, getting offended if you mispronounce their language or, God forbid, use English.

Within the first few hours of my first visit to Paris, I managed to bring a rain of French rudeness down upon myself by being confused about where the Metro ended and the Gare de Lyon began. I stumbled out of the Metro train, young, confused, on my first solo international trip. Exiting the Metro station for the train station proper – or so I thought – I finally tracked

---

[1] If we're still in Iraq in the year 2102, I, for one, think it would be time to consider a "cut-and-run" strategy.

down a ticket counter, where I attempted to purchase a ticket to Genoa, Italy.

Bonjour, parlez-vous Anglais? I said. See? I was doing everything right. I even used the formal tense. The man nodded his head in the affirmative. *Great, I'd like to buy a train ticket to Genoa.* The ticket man feigned an exaggerated confused look. *I don't understand,* he said, *what is 'Genoa?'* I didn't know how to respond to this. Genoa is a major city in Northern Italy – less than 500 miles away as the crow flies – surely he had heard of it? *Um, it's a city?* I ventured. No response. *It's in Italy... on the Italian Riviera? Genoa. Does the train go there?* He didn't reply; he just kept bugging his eyes out and shrugging as if he had no idea what I was talking about.

Finally another customer in the line tapped me on the shoulder and told me what the ticket seller wouldn't. *You're still in the tube!* It took me a moment to figure out what the hell he meant by "tube," then I blushed and quickly walked away, the ticket man still shaking his head with an incredulous look on his face.

From that moment on, I was terrified to so much as speak in Paris. Sure, I'd studied French, I could conjugate a few verbs and form a complete sentence or two. But what if I misspoke? Would there be more sarcastic eye-rolling? Or worse, what if I committed some dreadful social *faux pas*, like asking for ketchup? Would I be publicly humiliated again?

Luckily I managed to avoid any further embarrassment, and soon I found myself in Italy, where on more than one occasion I began speaking Italian only to be stopped and asked to continue in English *because they liked hearing my American accent so much.* Take that, Frenchie!

Of course, now Barack Obama is president and the rest of the world seems to like us again, so I guess this whole chapter is moot. Feel free to travel to just about any country in the world without worrying about the consequences – you're more likely to collect high-fives than criticism. Ironically, travel *within* the States just got a little more complicated. I voted for Barack, but I'll be leaving my "Obama Said Knock You Out" and "No, We McCain't" T-shirts at home if I ever have to travel through the Bible Belt.

10. Livin' La Boca Loca

"Xeneize" is a word in the Genovese dialect that means, simply, "Genovese." Is it redundant and kind of silly to have a special word to refer to your own people that only your own people will truly understand? A little, but consider how George Bush pronounces the word "Americans[1]," and you'll see that the Italians aren't the only ones guilty of this linguistic indulgence.

In any case, Xeneize is pronounced "Zen-AY-say" in the Genovese dialect, and pretty similarly in the La Boca neighborhood in Buenos Aires, Argentina[2]. See, the neighborhood was formed when thousands of Italian immigrants, mostly from Genoa, arrived in Buenos Aires looking for work. Having moved from one port city to another, most of them found jobs down at the dock, and La Boca slowly grew out of the brightly colored shipping containers many of them appropriated and slapped together as ramshackle housing.

Why the history lesson? Well, it turns out I have a pretty strong connection to Buenos Aires that I never knew about. My father, and his father, were both born in Genoa, Italy. But my grandfather's parents – my great-grandparents – were born in Buenos Aires. Apparently their parents (my great-great-grandparents) were among the many Xeniezes who emigrated from Italy to Argentina before the turn of the century. But for some reason, they moved back to Italy before conceiving my grandfather, which is why today

---

[1] 'Mericans.
[2] If you want to pronounce it perfectly in Argentina, substitute the "j" sound from "Taj Mahal" for the "x" in "xeneize."

I'm your average West Coast half-Italian, half-Anglo (IE: WASPy) guy, instead of Manu Ginobili.

Now, I love Italian food and culture, and, as mentioned, I've been to Italy several times. But I'm not, say, Jonathan Safran Foer – I didn't embark on this trip to learn more about my family's heritage and then write an alternately humorous and agonizingly post-modern book about it. No. Remember, I hate that shit. I came on this trip to eat great food and sit on the beach. And also because my wife made me. Remember that.

Rather, it was sheer coincidence (and the fact that they have wonderful steak at a reasonable price) that brought us to Argentina. It wasn't until the end of our time in Buenos Aires – after we'd already visited the La Boca neighborhood – that my father decided to casually mention that his grandparents had been born there.

Now, if I were so inclined, I could glom onto this newly discovered cultural background and claim it as my own. After all, there's a lot to like about Argentina and Buenos Aires specifically – and I'm not only referring to the steak. The *porteños,* as residents of Buenos Aires are known, have a laid-back European lifestyle going on that is quite enviable. Consider an average day: Wake at 11, café from 12 to 3, afternoon nap, perhaps a glass of wine and an appetizer with friends from 5 to 7, evening nap, dinner at 11, the club at 2.

I'm half joking. The *porteños* don't take two naps per day. But they do spend an incredible amount of time sipping *café con leche* and looking cool at alfresco cafés and they absolutely do go out to dinner at 11pm (or later).

Even if I wanted to be a cultural pretender, I simply can't hang with the Argentines. With a nap I might make it to 11pm before drowsing off, but there's no way I'd be able to sit down to a massive *parilla*[1] at that hour and then follow it up with a night out at the clubs.

And while this Argentinean pseudo-Euro lifestyle is fabulous, not all neighborhoods in Buenos Aires were created equal. Palermo, Recoleta, Belgrano and even crumbling old San Telmo are packed with trendy restaurants and boutique shops, but La Boca is different. It's poor, dirty, dangerous and decidedly un-glamorous. If I wanted to "represent" Buenos Aires in the sense that a rapper "represents" his neighborhood, I'd be stuck with the stevedores down in gritty La Boca rather than hobnobbing with the beautiful people in Palermo Hollywood.

Ah, but La Boca does have something the other neighborhoods lack – *La Bombonera*. Spanish for "chocolate box," *La Bombonera* is the nickname commonly used for the Estadio Alberto J. Armando, a stadium in the heart of the La Boca neighborhood and home to one of the most notorious soccer teams in the world – the Boca Juniors.

Soccer, you say? *Why, that's the most boring professional sport in America!* Yes, in America, soccer is what you play when you're not good enough for Pee-Wee football or Little League. In our country, it's a safe sport that doesn't humiliate the less-talented kids. Anxious soccer moms don't have to watch their kid strike out or get bowled over by a larger child like they might in basketball or football.

However, in other countries, soccer is kind of a big deal. People literally live and die by the results of the games, and that kind of competitive fire trickles down to the lowest levels of the sport. Substitute your average 8 year-old American kid with shin guards into a game anywhere else in the world and he will be

---

[1] Barbecue.

dominated and humiliated – and he certainly won't get a consolation orange slice or trip to McDonald's afterward.

Of course, the same things that make soccer safe for kids in the U.S. are what doom it to fail at the professional level in our country. By the time American kids reach high school, the ones with real athletic talent invariably move on from soccer to more popular sports like basketball, baseball and football, and the less-talented ones move on to band, math and Call of Duty 4.

Additionally, we have little soccer tradition and no real soccer stars in America – and we really hate games that can end in a tie, like hockey – so why should we give a damn about the game? That's a rhetorical question; don't bother answering. Not only do Americans not care about professional soccer, we can't seem to understand why anyone would.

Still, soccer is *the* sport in most of the rest of the world, except for China, where it's ping-pong. And no matter how poor or down-on-its-luck a particular country or city is, the fans always support their team in true soccer fashion: by behaving like complete fucking maniacs. If that team also happens to be good, look out, because those fans are going to be the craziest of the crazies[1].

Of all the teams in the world, the Boca Juniors might be the best manifestation of this theory. Their fans are largely the poor, working-class immigrants that populate La Boca. They have two nicknames for themselves: *Los Xeneizes,* which we've already discussed, and *Los Bosteros,* which roughly translates to "shit-shovelers," in reference to the manure factory

---

[1] In 1978, Argentina was run by a military dictatorship that "disappeared" an estimated 30,000 dissidents. But they also won the World Cup that year, so it's all good.

that formerly occupied the stadium grounds. Pardon me while I borrow some dialect from Larry the Cable Guy: *It don't git much more redneck than that.*

And the team is damn good. They've won as many international titles as AC Milan, the multi-million dollar club from Serie A, the Italian league. They produced Diego Maradona, the Argentine footballer who famously scored back-to-back goals in the 1986 World Cup (which were later nicknamed the "Hand of God" goal and the "Goal of the Century.") And they routinely beat their biggest rivals – River Plate, a team that represents the chichi neighborhood of Nuñez – in a matchup that makes a tidy little metaphor for Argentina's class struggles.

Great team... obsessive fans with nothing to lose... it's the perfect storm. If you thought a "soccer riot" was what happened when the coach of your kid's team didn't bring enough trophies for everyone, then you haven't been to a match in Latin America. Soccer riots in the third world are the real deal, with tear gas, Molotov cocktails, overturned vehicles and the occasional knifing. And while Buenos Aires might seem too developed and civilized to play host to such a fiasco, quite the opposite is true. The *Xeneizes* frequently turn their neighborhood into a war zone following a disappointing or controversial game, going to far as to hunt down fans of the opposing team[1].

Still, if there were any single aspect of Argentinean culture I might want to appropriate given my newly-discovered heritage, Boca Junior fandom might just be it. Hey, my family was from this

---

[1] This has happened often enough to prompt a new security rule. As the game is winding down, riot police move into place and literally block the Boca supporters from leaving the stadium, allowing opposing fans, players and coaches a full 20 minutes to escape.

neighborhood! I could become a legitimate supporter of the *Xeneizes*. All I needed to do was learn a few of the players' names, buy a jersey, maybe catch a game or two on TV, right?

Wrong. Even though she hates watching sports on TV and couldn't care less about going to a Blazers or Seahawks game back home, Liz became obsessed with seeing a Boca game in person. She doesn't give a damn about soccer, mind you, but she loves danger. If there's a chance we'll be trampled to death and/or tear-gassed, she'll be first in line.

I waffled on this one a bit. On the one hand, I would have felt a bit of a poseur wearing a Boca jersey never having seen the team in person. On the other hand, I avoid riots as a general rule, and there had been a fairly major one at the Boca game the week before, resulting in more than 100 arrests and at least one stabbing.

Of course, there was an alternative. Despite the well-publicized danger, Boca Juniors games are a major tourist draw, and most of the youth hostels around town offer chaperoned package deals, in which a bona fide local ushers a group of nervous tourists into a special section to enjoy the game away from the drunken, crazy La Boca locals.

Normally if there are two ways to do something, and one of them is far more dangerous than the other, I opt for the safer choice. However, the only thing I might enjoy more than safety is not spending money. The chaperoned package cost around $80 per ticket, whereas a single ticket in the crazy, drunken section could be had for under $10. I had a decision to make – spend the dough and eliminate most of the risk, or save a few bucks and potentially get knifed. It was a closer call than you can imagine.

At the last minute, a third option presented itself. A fellow traveler told us that we could head down to *La Bombonera* independently and buy our own tickets for the special tourist section. Apparently they only cost $25 or so... the hostels were taking advantage of tourist paranoia and jacking up the rates. Save money *and* avoid a tear gassing by the riot police? Count me in.

On the public bus ride over I mustered my best hardened adventurer face. I mean, we *had* been traveling for six months already – we should have been confident. *Don't fuck with me, pal; I've been to Cambodia.* We disembarked on a run-down street corner and nonchalantly tried to figure out where to go, soon deciding to follow a group of raggedy kids through a grass field riddled with broken grass bottles. Yeah, it sounds sketchy, but we saw the top of the blue-and-yellow *Bombonera* in the background and figured it was a shortcut.

After passing two security checkpoints we located the ticket box office and attempted to purchase seats, only to be told that the special tourist section was full. Did we want to purchase tickets for the regular Boca section? Even Liz wasn't sure about this. This was the section at the end of the stadium reserved for the wildest, poorest fans – the ones who couldn't afford more than a couple bucks for a ticket, but who would rather kill themselves than miss a game.

We took a step back to think about it. I mean, we were already there, we had our game faces on, did we really want to chicken out and hop on a bus back to our cozy apartment to watch the game on TV? Just as we were pondering our options, we noticed another American couple in the same situation. They had approached the adjacent ticket window simultaneously only to retreat without tickets, just as we had.

We introduced ourselves, compared stories, and then all had the same thought simultaneously: What if the four of us bought tickets for the crazy section and just stuck together? Four gringos are surely safer than two? Live together, die alone, right? After a few minutes, and a few deep breaths, it was decided. We'd all get the cheap tickets, under the condition that we would stick together at all times, and that we would leave as a group if any of us felt things getting out of control.

Having a couple of American companions was somehow reassuring, even if, when push came to shove, they couldn't possibly be of much assistance – the guy was built about like me (a touch skinnyfat) and his girlfriend couldn't have been an ounce over 95 pounds. Nevertheless, we soldiered on, buoyed by a false sense of security, stopping briefly to wolf down a few *choripan*[1] from a street vendor and to purchase a counterfeit Boca jersey.

Simply entering *La Bombonera* is a daunting task. First you have to figure out which entrance to use, which means wandering among the rambunctious Boca streets until you find the right one. Then you must pass multiple security points where you will be repeatedly frisked and forced to surrender any liquids. Hey, it's just like flying. Another similarity to flying: I couldn't decide if all the heightened security made me more or less confident about my chances of survival.

Finally, we made it. Away from all the armed security battalions and fans still lubricating themselves with Quilmes beer out in the streets, the stadium entryway was eerily deserted. We faced a long, winding path up to the second level – plenty of time to second-guess what we were getting ourselves into.

At that moment, I felt more like a Roman gladiator than I ever had before, and probably ever will

---

[1] Sausage and bread. Basically, the Argentinean equivalent of a Dodger Dog.

again[1]. We could hear far-off chanting, and the tunnel was vibrating with the force of thousands of fans stomping their feet and jumping up and down. *Those about to die, we salute you.* We walked four abreast through the empty pathway, all of us looking around nervously, not sure what to expect once we finally broke through into the open.

Fortunately for me as a person (but unfortunately for me as an author), our arrival – and the game itself – were completely anti-climactic. We popped out of the tunnel to find an average looking stadium filled with mostly reasonable-looking people enjoying *choripan* and Coke while occasionally bursting into an amazingly coordinated chant. Nobody tried to pickpocket or molest us and I was even able to sneak my digital camera out into the open for a few pictures, something the guide books warn against doing.

The only tense moments came at the end of the game, when dozens of burly security guards arrived to block us from leaving the stadium. The Juniors had won the match handily against an inferior opponent, so everyone was relatively happy, but nobody enjoys being confined for very long and the mood was getting darker by the minute. Just when I thought it couldn't get any sweatier or crowded without a scuffle breaking out, the guards parted and allowed us to disperse. Whew.

It wasn't until later that I realized just how fortunate our timing was. A lot of people claim that the safest time to do something is directly after a major tragedy. You know, like flying on September 12, 2001.

---

[1] A close second would be the first time I played blackjack at Caesar's Palace as a 21 year-old Vegas newbie and actually managed to win money. I'd like to think I walked away from the table in slow motion and shouted, "Are you not entertained??!!!??!" But that probably didn't happen.

Or eating at Jack in the Box after that E. Coli outbreak. You figure that all the negative attention creates an atmosphere in which it would be unthinkable for the same mistakes to happen again. In our case, we attended the first game directly after what turned out to be the biggest riot of the season. Also, it was on Easter Sunday, and it simply wouldn't do for the deeply religious *Xeneizes* to spend such an important holy day in prison.

Yep, it had all worked out pretty nicely. Liz got to enjoy the anticipation of real danger, while I was thrilled to avoid any actual threat to my well-being. We met some new friends, with whom we shared a pitcher of Quilmes in Plaza Dorrego later that night. And, having been to a game, I can now wear my Boca jersey with the custom iron-on *"Xeneizes"* logo on the back with something approaching pride. Or at least less shame.

Of course, danger is everywhere, and if you're going to travel all the way around the world through a bunch of backwater countries, there's simply no way to avoid it entirely. But by the time we made it to Argentina, I was wary of voluntarily signing myself up for *extra* danger, as we repeatedly had in Southeast Asia.

11. Better Trek Through the Jungle

In addition to cockroaches, ladyboys, counterfeit Rolexes and drunken British ex-pats, death-defying jungle treks seem to be an integral part of any Thailand experience. After completing our own adventure, we compared stories with many other travelers and found a shocking number of common themes, including but not limited to:

- Large and/or poisonous insects.
- Unprepared guides
- Rickety bridges
- Abject terror

Needless to say, I didn't know what we were in for ahead of time, and if Liz knew, she sure didn't tell me. I was already terrified enough of Southeast Asia as it was. Although I now know it would have been a huge mistake, I would have been happy to skip Asia completely.

Liz, thankfully, didn't let this happen. Asia was always a deal breaker. If I didn't want to go, she would go by herself. I could hang out in whatever country I liked while she walked right into the heart of darkness. She knew that *that* would make me more nervous than anything we'd actually encounter, and she was right. So when it came time to book our tickets, I gulped and agreed to three and a half months split between Thailand, Laos, Vietnam and Cambodia.

Still, as our time in Italy ran out, I began to dread the next leg on our journey. What had I gotten myself into? I pictured dirty, dusty streets filled with beggars and rabid dogs. Thousands of tiny, desperate hands clawing at me for spare change every time I disembarked from a bus. And my guts churned with the ever-present fear of being framed for drug-smuggling and sent to prison for the rest of my life, or executed. Thanks, *Brokedown Palace.*

So you can imagine my surprise when we arrived in Bangkok and were promptly whisked to our guest house in an SUV taxi that was far nicer than any vehicle I've ever owned. Through the window, all I could see were endless overpasses and billboards. Whoa, it was like a real city!

And then we arrived at our guest house. Oh, it was lovely. A private room with ice-cold AC and a massive bed made up with soft, clean, white sheets. Wireless internet. No cockroaches (yet). I walked through the tranquil common area in a dream, taking in the pleasant scent of incense and spicy food being prepared nearby. I didn't yet know that this would be the second-nicest place (by far) that we would stay for the next three months, but I had an inkling, so I took as much advantage as I could.

I didn't want to leave. The room only cost $21 per night (I hadn't yet realized that this is actually a fortune in Thailand)... *Hey, let's just spend a couple weeks here!* Liz wouldn't hear it. She was okay with staying four or five nights to adjust to the new time zone and to get used to an entirely new diet, but by the last day or two, I could tell she was getting restless.

So, with a little help from our resident friend, we decided to head north, to a town called Mae Sot right next to the Burmese border. From there, we'd take a small truck, called a *song tau*, about six hours to a tiny village called Um Phang (pronounced "oom-pong"). It was supposed to be a great launching point for all kinds of outdoor adventures.

The moment we boarded that first overnight bus to Mae Sot marked our transition from cozy, fancy traveling to real down and dirty backpacking. No more plush hotel rooms or bilingual tour guides; now we'd have to make our own way with perhaps five words of Thai and our own street sense, which was put immediately to use when we were unceremoniously dropped off in the middle of nowhere at 4am. Still groggy from the few hours of half-sleep we'd managed to grab, we didn't believe the bus driver when he said we'd arrived in Mae Sot. I remembered stopping for extended periods during the night at various checkpoints, the bus laboring up steep hills at a crawl before careening violently through dozens of hairpin curves. So how, exactly, did we manage to beat our estimated arrival time by four hours?

We never found out. The bus continued north, leaving us in a desolate terminal with a handful of tuk-tuk drivers dozing away in their chariots. We woke one and asked for a ride into town, to the Green Guest House. He hadn't heard of that specific place, but he had a general idea where it was, so off we went. He dropped us near a bridge over some of the most stagnant, filthy water I've ever seen. I sat on my bag, reapplying mosquito repellent and cursing under my breath while Liz scouted the area to see if anyone was awake.

And, miracle of miracles, someone was. Our driver had only overshot the Green Guest House by a block or so. A kind Thai woman led us inside the gates and explained that there was only a single vacant bed remaining in a three-bed dorm. That was good enough for us at 4am after a tortured night of pitching back and forth in the magical mystery bus, so we agreed to the bed sight unseen.

Of course, when she quietly opened the door and turned on the light, we discovered that our bed was about three feet from the bed of an enormous fat man, naked save a pair of stained boxers, who had vomited during the night and was presently tossing and turning in said vomit. The Thai lady ever so slightly shook her head disapprovingly, then gave us a little shrug, as if to say, *take it or leave it.*

We took it. I shut my eyes and the next thing I knew it was 11am and the room was empty. No sign of the puke-stained whale or his filthy sheets. I stumbled outside and found Liz waiting for me, casually sipping a soda water and reading her book. Mercifully, we decided to spend another night recuperating in Mae Sot before trying to get to Um Phang. After changing rooms, of course.

The next morning, we gathered our things and marched through the blisteringly hot streets in search of our *song tau* stop. After a little backtracking we finally found it; an unmarked (in English, anyway) little open-air office with several people already waiting for the next truck. We looked to be about seventh or eighth in line; I hoped there'd be room for us.

We needn't have worried. When the *song tau* pulled up, we were waved to the front of the line. We deferred, but they insisted. We heard the word *falang* tossed about a few times. It basically means "whitey," but English-speaking Thai swear up and down that it doesn't have a negative connotation. In this case, they wanted to make sure that the *falang* had proper seats in the *song tau*. Generally, only Thai passengers (or experienced, Thai-speaking *falang*) are allowed to ride on the roof or standing up at the rear of the vehicle.

A more thorough description of what exactly a *song tau* looks like is probably in order. First, picture an average two-door pickup truck with 400,000 miles on it. Now, imagine that someone has welded a steel cage canopy atop the bed and installed two benches on the inside. That's pretty much it. Appropriately, the name *song tau* literally means "two benches." There's also usually a crude luggage rack atop the canopy, and the cage often extends slightly beyond the rear of the original cab to accommodate standing room only passengers, who put their feet on the rails and hang on for dear life.

After tossing our larger backpacks onto the roof, we clambered in and sat opposite one another. There was one passenger already in the truck; a young girl sitting on my side, facing away from us as we entered. I tried to give her plenty of space, but soon realized there was none to spare as more as more passengers wedged themselves in. With about 10 people in the *song tau*, I figured we were ready to roll. Then the operators placed a ramp on the edge of the bed and began rolling a motorbike towards it. They couldn't possibly be thinking of loading a fucking motorcycle into the back of this thing, could they?

Evidently they could. The driver and an assistant cheerfully rolled the bike up the ramp and halfway into the bed, poking people in the knees, then tied the bike somewhat securely into place. For good measure they added two more standing passengers on each side, and placed a young child atop the motorbike's seat. A final passenger stood straddling the bike just behind the boy. And we were off.

Now, there were two important pieces of information I was not aware of when we planned this jungle trek. The first is that I would be mashed into the back of a truck with 14 other people and a motorcycle for the duration of the ride. It was uncomfortable, but I'd done worse. The *Trenitalia* ride to Florence was worse, as was the time I had to ride in the cab of a tow truck in the middle of Montana with six people. (I got stuck next to the driver and every time he needed to shift gears, he had to reach between my legs. Good times.)

But the second piece of information was more sinister. I could deal with the discomfort, but I was really rather unhappy to learn later that the road we had just endured for six hours was nicknamed "Death Highway."

Ah, but Liz insisted that the road wasn't called Death Highway because so many people died while driving on it (although they had, and still do); it was called Death Highway because of all the Burmese refugee camps that line the road. Apparently there has been a lot of blood spilled in the many battles and border disputes along that particular stretch of road, not to mention the sad conditions and death associated with the camps themselves. *See, it's just named Death Highway because of all the killings. Not the highway deaths. The killings!* I felt so much better.

The ride was preposterously dangerous. The driver cut every corner like he was racing around Monte Carlo in a Formula 1 car. We barely dodged oncoming traffic, huge piles of gravel and cracks in the road. We'd fly downhill, banking the corner, then swoop up wildly around another bend just along the edge of a cliff. But, I have to admit, the driver had skills. He didn't ride the brakes; he used the engine masterfully to cut velocity when needed. Even though this was probably the most dangerous road we'd travel on our entire trip, the bus drivers in Vietnam made me far more nervous.

Death Highway conquered, we arrived in Um Phang six hours later. We found a decent enough place to stay, but we still weren't sure what kind of trek we were going to do. There were a lot of options. You can visit a village populated by the indigenous Karen people. You can ride elephants. You can swim in a waterfall. And you can go river rafting. There are half a dozen tour companies that offer all of these options and more, in varying combinations. We were stuck, flooded with an overabundance of choices.

And then we ran into another American couple at our guest house, Gavin and Emily. From Seattle! It was refreshing to talk to people with the same non-accent as us. They mentioned that they were probably going to do a trek the next day, and recommended a particular tour office before heading out to zip around town on their motorbike. By the time they got back, Liz and I had reached a decision: We were going to beg them to allow us to tag along. Luckily we didn't have to get on our knees; they were happy to have us.

That night we picked up a couple bottles of booze. Sang Som Thai Rum and a bottle of Mekong Whisky that the store owner advised against purchasing (ominously, he called it "magic water"). Then we played cards, had dinner and got to know each other. Maybe it was magic water, or the heat coming off the spicy food, but we didn't really notice how cold it was becoming. We laughed it up until it was time to hit the sack, at which point we noticed it was pretty close to freezing.

Of course, Liz and I had left our sweaters and warm gear back in Bangkok with our friend. All we had were a couple flimsy blankets provided by the guest house and our own paper-thin sleep sheets. It was a terrible night, and suddenly we remembered that we'd be spending the next two nights sleeping under the stars during our three-day trek. The next morning, with only a few minutes to spare before we were supposed to embark, Liz and I rushed into the town in search of warmer clothes. This being Thailand, even a "cold" part of Thailand, the pickings were slim. I chose an extremely scratchy fake wool hat with a fake Liverpool logo on it (Liz got one that read "Beckham") and the largest gloves they had in stock, which would have fit me perfectly when I was 12.

Marginally better prepared, still sore from our restless night, we hurried back to the tour office and attempted to "pack" for the journey. Packing in this case involving unpacking. We had to take all the stuff we weren't going to need and leave it behind in Um Phang. It was a lot harder than it should have been, as we couldn't get a clear answer from the guides as to what exactly we'd need. This would become a common theme among our various treks, tours and activities throughout Southeast Asia. Ultimately we all brought way too much stuff and got off to a late start. In other words, it was completely standard.

We had two tour guides. The first, Victor, was a boyish Burmese man who could have been anywhere between 16 and 35 years old. We had no idea. He didn't have any facial hair, but claimed that he could grow a beard if he wanted. Apparently he preferred the clean shaven look, because he told Gavin – a white guy with a thick brown beard – that he looked like Osama Bin Laden.

Johnny was our other guide, a smiling, sneering rugged little guy who looked grizzled enough – and had enough skill with a machete – to make us think he'd probably seen some sort of military action in his day. We were pretty sure he wasn't Thai either.

They were both friendly – and Johnny in particular seemed experienced and knowledgeable – but neither spoke English particularly well. Like many tour guides, they had a basic grasp of the language and had obviously memorized certain key speeches, but they also tended to blurt out exceedingly important instructions in nervous, mumbled torrents. *Helloladiesandgentlemens, wegoriverraftingnow, pleaseputonlifevestandavoiddeadlyeelsthankyouvery much.*

Still, the first day of the trek was laughably easy, and we began to wonder what exactly we'd signed up for. After all, Johnny and Victor did all the paddling and steering as we rafted down the river, they pitched our tents, they cooked our lunch and dinner and they cleaned up after us. We felt like babies. And then there was our campsite. Far from being the tiny clearing hacked out of the heart of the jungle that I pictured, it was more like a KOA on a 4th of July weekend.

There were hundreds of tents, and perhaps over a thousand people. All Thai – we didn't meet any other Westerners. Turns out it was a major holiday weekend in Thailand, and our campsite happened to be one of the most popular vacation spots in the country.

We all joked again about how much of a cakewalk this was turning out to be, then followed Victor and Johnny along a ridiculously manicured path to the campsite's main attraction: the Tee Lor Su waterfall. Again, it was easy, pleasant, relaxing. We smiled and said *sawadee khrap*[1] to aging grandmothers, little kids, people in wheelchairs, then hustled back to camp to face the only real challenge of the day: finding something to drink.

All the Thais had come prepared; we were empty-handed. Gavin and I walked the perimeter of the camp, asking anyone who looked even remotely official if there was any alcohol for sale. Finally we found a lady who said she could help us out.

"What you want, beer, whisky, rum?"

"Yes."

"Which one?"

"Any of it. All of it. Whatever you've got."

Our choice was made simple when we followed her to the booze dispensary and discovered that there was only a single large bottle of Sang Som remaining in the entire campsite. We gladly forked over whatever they were charging and got down to some serious drinking.

---

[1] "Hello," if you're a guy. *Sawadee kah* if you're a girl.

That night was one of the most peaceful nights of sleep I had in Thailand. I was warm and cozy in my Liverpool hat and four shirts, secure in the knowledge that we were going to survive this jungle trek, and just the right amount of drunk.

After breakfast the next morning, we grilled Victor about the day's activities. *We go to see waterfall, then hike, later on, swim.* But Victor, we already saw the waterfall. *No, we go up.* We didn't know what he meant. He shrugged and we all waited for Johnny to show up and explain. Five minutes later, Johnny swaggered into view carrying an extremely large machete. *You wan' hike to top of waterfall?* Hell yes we did.

Finally, some adventure. Johnny hid the machete in the back of his waistband and we all walked to the trailhead checkpoint. He and Victor chatted up the guards for a moment, and I noticed all the park regulations for the first time. No exiting the path. No removing flora or fauna from the park. No smoking. No machetes. Little did we know we were about to flaunt each of these regulations.

About halfway along the official manicured path, Johnny and Victor stopped, looked both ways, then darted off into the jungle and motioned for us to follow. This was the start of the unofficial path, the one that would climb nearly 200 meters over the course of perhaps one and a half kilometers to the summit of Tee Lor Su. The one that was known only to Burmese jungle warriors and their lucky American foot soldiers.

Johnny bushwhacked like an expert and we did our best to keep up. It was steep and muddy, and I was wearing a pair of Nike skate shoes. At one point I slipped and fell pretty hard, nearly sliding out of control off the path. *Careful*, I heard either Johnny or Victor yell from the lead. They were both wearing flip flops.

We came to a resting point. Johnny whipped out his machete and grinned. If he was going to murder us, he picked a good time to do it; all us *falang* were sucking wind. Instead, he started hacking away at some bamboo, chopping down a large section and then carefully whittling it into smaller pieces. *What your name?* he asked, pointing at Liz. *Liz*, she replied. He carved "Lic" onto the side of one of the bamboo pieces. He repeated the process, finally handing us each a crude bamboo cup with some semblance of our name on it. *For drink beer later.* Oh my God, yes!

Bamboo beer mugs in hand, we continued our ascent. We reached the summit, then had to pick our way carefully across hundreds of deep pools to reach the edge of the waterfall. And suddenly, we were there. The top of Tee Lor Su. The water wasn't terribly deep or swift; you could walk right through it, as close to the edge as you dared. Victor perched on a rock and looked bored while Johnny climbed a massive tree and smoked a cigarette, staring down at us with amused detachment.

We all crept as close to the edge as we could without freaking out. From that point, we could actually see tourists at the base of the waterfall, looking up at us. We smiled, waved, flipped them off, took pictures. Then Johnny came down from his tree and it was time to go.

Back at base camp we had lunch and readied our gear for the next stage of the journey: hiking to the Karen village. Johnny had another obligation to attend to (perhaps a military coup?) so it would just be the four of us and Victor. And this time we would have to carry our own packs in addition to all the extra sleeping bags we had requested to keep warm.

In spite of the extra weight and several unexpectedly sketchy bamboo bridges, we made it to the Karen village in time for a quick dip at the swimming hole before sundown. This was the "waterfall swimming" that was supposed to be a highlight of the tour, and it actually was pretty amazing[1]. We swam across the milky blue channel to a sparkling multi-tiered structure that was part waterfall and part cave. It was almost too good to be true... kind of like we were swimming in a man-made fountain in Vegas. I half-expected security to throw me out at any moment.

Refreshed and relatively clean (none of us had dared shower in the disgusting Tee Lor Su facilities), we returned to the village and met up with the other tourists that we'd be sharing dinner with. They were:

Opart – A Thai restaurateur in his 50s from Mae Sot who had lived in Chicago for a number of years.

The Italian John Locke – Some guy from La Spezia who looked exactly like John Locke from *Lost*.

The Italian John Locke's Thai Wife – A cute Thai lady who'd recently gotten hitched to the enigmatic Mr. Locke. JLTW for short.

---

[1] It would have been even more amazing if we weren't collectively freezing our tits off, but what are you going to do? Actually get started on time? Unpossible. In Asia, if your tour isn't running at least an hour late, something is seriously amiss. You can set your watch by the roosters crowing at dawn and the Laotians hocking up loogies for a solid half hour immediately thereafter, and that's about it.

The seven of us sat in a circle on the floor and lit candles as Opart's personal chefs (and Victor, our personal chef, I guess), brought in plates of food. Opart kindly described each dish and how it was prepared, though he said he "couldn't vouch for" any of Victor's creations.

We all ate furiously, using sticky rice to pick up handfuls of chicken, beef and vegetables, slurping bowls of scalding-hot soup and trying to wash down the intense spice with lukewarm Beer Chang[1]. As dinner wound down, conversation hit a lull. The fact was, we had some serious language barriers to overcome. Usually everyone speaks English in these situations, but the Italian John Locke and JLTW couldn't hold their own[2]. By the time Victor joined us, we had people speaking in broken Italian (me), fluent Italian (John Locke) rapid-fire Thai (JLTW and Opart), Burmese-accented Thai (Victor), Thai-accented English (Opart), flat-out busted English (John Locke, JLTW and Victor) and broadcast English (all of us from the Pacific Northwest). Liz, Gavin and Emily also spoke Spanish, which, of course, was completely useless at the time.

But gambling is truly the universal language, so when Gavin pulled out a handful of dice and taught us a game called "threes," we were suddenly laughing it up and having a grand old time as if we'd all known each other for years. It should be pointed out that while we all enjoyed the game (except for Opart, who rolled once and then excused himself, seeming mildly offended), Victor and JLTW absolutely *loved* it. We weren't playing for real money – just for fun – but they

---

[1] In case you were wondering, our new bamboo beer mugs imparted a slightly fruity, tropical taste to the beer but also caused it to foam uncontrollably.

[2] The Italian John Locke didn't speak Thai. His wife didn't speak Italian. Neither of them spoke much English. Way to go, John!

whooped and hollered when they won and developed special shaking and blowing rituals for good luck before throwing the dice. I think I saw a few extra beads of sweat form on John Locke's brow when he got an eyeful of just how excited his new bride was about gambling games.

As fun as the game was, all the hiking and swimming had taken their toll. We didn't even make it through all the Beer Chang before retreating to our own hut for some sleep, though we wouldn't get much. Under mosquito nets and multiple sleeping bags, the bugs weren't bad. But the noise was unbearable. The village was louder at night than it was during the daytime. Dogs howled, chickens squawked and at one point I awoke from a bizarre dream about making homemade Nutter Butter cookies to what sounded like a pig eating our shoes. We'd left them outside to dry, and I was certain only scraps would remain in the morning.

When dawn finally broke I was startled out of sleep once again, this time by what sounded like an even larger animal – probably eating the pigs that had eaten our shoes[1]. A massive noise, unexplainable. I threw the covers off my head and looked up to see two elephants poking their heads into the hut next door. They were all geared up for passengers, with chains around their necks and seats straddling their backs. Then Opart and his crew popped their heads out and waved. They were his elephants. Since we'd opted out of elephant-riding, we'd be doing all our own walking for the rest of the trek.

And, excessive gear once again packed and loaded on our backs, walk we did. We were running

---

[1] Ultimately it turned out that our shoes had not actually been eaten by pigs.

late[1], so Victor set a grueling pace that left us sweating and red-faced at each break. We climbed up steep hills using exposed roots for traction, fought through deep mud and crossed several more laughably unsafe bamboo bridges. At one point our path merged with the elephant trail and we had to make our way among the two foot deep divots the elephants had gouged out of the mud. I had made the unfortunate fashion choice of wearing socks with my sandals (I know, I know, but my heels were blistered and bleeding), and when I accidentally stepped into one of the divots, I sunk to my calf and lost one of the socks forever.

Finally we reached the highest point and began descending. Catching my breath, I approached Victor to see what else was in store. *Almost done. We finish hike, then go swimming.* Oh, more swimming? Is it another waterfall? *No, swimming across river.* We're swimming across a river? How are we going to do that with our bags?

At this point Victor mimed holding a backpack above his head. I laughed and fell back in line with the others. Must not be a very deep river, I thought to myself, since Victor's only about 4'10". I wouldn't have to wait long to find out. Around half an hour later, we scampered down a long sandy bank and saw the river for ourselves.

"Oh," I said.

"Shit," Gavin added, finishing my thought.

The river was uncrossable. I'm not much of an outdoorsman, but I know what I know. It was swift, deep and a good 50 feet across. Victor was more likely to play in the NBA than he was to successfully walk across this thing. But, he appeared ready to give it a try, stripping down to his underwear and hoisting his bag above his head. Gavin, a former lifeguard, also got

---

[1] Duh.

down to his swim gear and prepared to save Victor, just in case.

We all stood transfixed as Victor waded in, the water quickly reaching his thighs, his hips, his chest. He was only a third of the way across. But then it seemed to flatten out and he took several steps without getting any deeper. *Maybe he's going to make it,* someone said.

A few steps later he sunk precipitously to his neck, but still kept straining against the current, holding his backpack mere inches above the water by now. And then, one step too many. His head and arms disappeared completely below the water, the backpack splashing into the current audibly. Gavin readied himself to dive in, but Victor popped back up in a flash, swimming now, clearly upset. He reigned in his backpack and quickly swam the rest of the way across.

On the other side he cursed and started tearing through his gear. Apparently he had some kind of an electronic language translator that had gotten wet. I felt bad for him, but I was still wondering how we were supposed to get across with all our gear. We had a digital camera, months of prescription medications, notebooks, journals, you name it. Heaps of stuff that just couldn't get wet, and only a single tiny dry bag to share between the four of us. It was like one of those goddamn riddles where you have like two llamas and two foxes and a raft, but you can't carry a llama and a fox at the same time and you have to figure out how to ford a river. God, I suck at those things.

As Liz, Emily and I tried to prioritize our possessions for the dry bag, Gavin and Victor held a shouted conversation across the river. Victor was suddenly very excited, pointing just downstream and gesturing for Gavin to head that direction. Following Victor's direction, Gavin disappeared into the brush.

Moments later we heard him shouting for us. *Hey guys, there's a raft over here!*

Salvation. Victor swam back across and got ready to ferry us to the other side. It was a long, skinny bamboo raft with a platform in the middle for passengers. Reassuringly, there was also a rope stretching across the river.

Still, I wasn't exactly sure how this was going to go down. The river was moving really fast – were we going to back the raft up a bit and let it carry us slightly downstream as we paddled across? Were we just going to pull ourselves across using the rope? Or what?

I started asking questions but Victor told me to relax and get on the boat. So, I did. Liz boarded as well, and we tossed several of the group's bags on board for good measure. As Victor started easing us out into the current, I whispered to Liz. *Keep your eye on that rope. If Victor starts losing control we'll need to grab it.*

We were perpendicular to the current. Victor stood near the front of the boat and pulled us forward, using a chain to anchor us to the rope. But within a few seconds, the current became too strong. We were sucked under the rope and Victor was left dangling between the rope and the raft, hanging on by a thread. *Grab the rope,* I shouted at Liz. We both seized the rope and hung on for dear life. And, between the three of us, we kept the raft from floating away downstream. Temporarily.

See, the dumb thing was that none of us really had an idea how to operate the raft, our tour guide included. To cross the river, you have to position the raft *parallel* to the current and gently ease it across. If you attempt to cross with the boat perpendicular to the current, one of two things will happen:

1. You will lose your grip on the rope and float away downstream.

or

2. You will hold on so tightly that the current will flow up and over the edge of your raft, causing it to flip.

I'm not sure which is worse, but we prevented the first outcome, leading to a dramatic realization of the second. The front edge dipped into the water, we held on even tighter, somewhere my former cub scout leader shook his head disapprovingly and tut-tutted, and that was all she wrote. We flipped the damn boat.

What happened next is a blur. Liz and I somehow got back onto the boat in a flash and rescued all our bags from floating away. I have no recollection as to how we did this. Meanwhile, Victor still hadn't lost his grip! He was somehow hanging onto the edge of the raft with his toes, suspended over the river. This was all that was keeping our whole operation from floating hundreds of yards downstream.

Meanwhile, Gavin dove into the river to our aid. He swam straightaway to the deepest, swiftest part and helped Victor regain control. Then, both immersed in the water, they guided us the rest of the way across. Of course by this point the boat had become parallel with the current, as it should have been all along, so it was much easier.

A few other guides had arrived on the far side of the river as our debacle was unfolding, and one of them ferried back across to get Emily and the rest of our stuff. He nonchalantly stood at the edge of the raft the whole time, expending less effort than one might reading a newspaper, as Liz, Victor and I dripped and seethed in the sun on the opposite shore. Only Gavin seemed chipper, perhaps stoked that he'd been able to put his lifeguard skills to good use.

If our entire jungle trek had been a game of Oregon Trail, culminating in the final challenge of a river crossing, I would have gotten dysentery and Liz would have lost all her bullets. It was a pretty epic failure. But thankfully it was real life, and the only real tragedy was that my newish notebook sustained a little water damage.

And we learned an important lesson: we suck at adventure. I mean, sure, we're up for swimming and hiking and mountain biking and other macho outdoor activities, but when the chips are down, and our asses are on the line, we're probably going to be the ones that get eaten by bears or fall off a cliff and have to be rescued by a rock-climbing Sylvester Stallone. We're just not cut out to be Eagle Scouts.

This probably helps explain why we spent so much time watching *Friends* in the middle of a Laotian jungle.

12. It's Like You're Always Stuck in Second Gear, Well It Hasn't Been Your Day, Your Week, Your Month or Even Your Year

Ah, the life lessons we can all learn from *Friends*. You don't even have to watch the show; the theme song alone is a mini therapy session. *Just relax*, the lyrics imply, *and your friends will get you through this rough patch*. Whether it's Chandler's unfortunate relationship with Janice, Rachel and Ross' on-again off-again romance or Joey's struggle to become a legitimate actor, each show is a thirty-minute conflict/resolution wrapped in a tidy package... with a little help from the protagonist's friends, of course.

Of all the cultures and ethnic groups we encountered on our trip, the uber-relaxed Lao people embodied this sitcom-friendly ethic to a tee. Sure, they want to sell you a tuk-tuk ride, but unlike their neighbors in Vietnam, they won't hunt you down and give you a twenty-minute sales pitch over a five-minute ride. Rather, they'll just wave their hand dismissively and go back to doing shots of Lao Lao rice whisky if you decline. Fun is more important than work to the Lao people – our Lonely Planet guidebook suggests that Laotians won't even consider a job that doesn't have some element of fun to it.

Why is this so? How could the Vietnamese and Lao people – so close geographically and ethnically – act so differently in their everyday dealings? The Vietnamese sell, sell, sell, the Laotians sleep, sleep, sleep. Some people claim that the Laotians have always been this way – that it's simply in their nature to be relaxed and mellow. Others cite their passivity as a cultural response to centuries of oppression and struggle.

My theory? There is a town in northern Laos that broadcasts *Friends* reruns around the clock from every single television in every single bar in town – it's pretty clear to me that the show is hypnotizing and brainwashing the entire country by osmosis.

Perhaps I should back up. The town I speak of is called Vang Vieng, and it's the middle stop on what has become a well-worn three part tourist trail through the heart of the country. To the south lies the urban capital of Vientiane, a moderately bustling city that was heavily influenced by French colonial rule. To the north, rustic Luang Prabang offers ancient temples and postcard-friendly views of the bordering Mekong River. Smack dab in the middle is Vang Vieng, the best place in Southeast Asia to get stoned out of your gourd on pot milkshakes and watch the episode where Joey gets his head stuck in a turkey.

In fact, pot-laced foods and *Friends* have become such staples in Vang Vieng that all the guidebooks mention the town's TV bars specifically. I know how bizarre this all sounds, and I was skeptical too. But once you wander the streets for yourself and witness hundreds of zonked-out backpackers kicking back on axe pillows, ordering round after round of Beer Lao and, in some cases, singing along with the theme song, there's no denying it's real.

Here's how it works. Just grab a seat at one of the dozens of TV bars that line most of Vang Vieng's streets. Take a look at the menu. Is there something called a "happy shake" that costs way more than an ordinary milkshake should? That's a pot milkshake, my friend. Don't miss the "happy pizza," an equally popular choice. Of course, if you don't see any "happy" items on your menu, it's possible that your particular TV bar doesn't sell drugs. But it's more likely that you simply have to ask for the special "happy menu," which should be loaded with plenty of delicious, discreet ways to help you turn on, tune in and drop out.

As for the *Friends* part of this strange equation, it's an unusual phenomenon, but one that I believe is easily explained using logic. See, Vang Vieng sits in the middle of one of the most stunning natural settings in all of Asia. Consequently, it is visited by armies of outdoorsy backpackers. And while outdoorsy backpackers enjoy hiking and biking and kayaking in and around the area's magnificent limestone cliffs, they also enjoy doing drugs, lying on pillows and watching TV directly *after* those sorts of activities. *Friends* is a no-brainer – the snappy, laugh-a-minute dialogue sucks you into episode after episode, and without any commercials to bring you back to reality it's easy to rip through half a season in a single setting.

Still not getting the appeal? Imagine that you're higher than the International Space Station and people keep bringing you food and milkshakes to munch on. Joey is wearing all of Chandler's clothes. Monica is wearing a fat suit. Rachel is going commando. Ross just fell down go boom. Ha, ha, ha, ha, ha, ha, ha. Ha. Ha. Ha. Do you see why it's so hard to get up once you sit down?

Now, I'm not just saying this because my friends and family and potential future employers are reading this book, but for all my talk of happy shakes in this chapter, Liz and I abstained from doing any drugs on our trip. My reasons for doing so should be obvious: I am the Reluctant Traveler, and I was scared to death of getting caught. There are two possible punishments for crossing the Thai border with drugs on your person: Life in prison or death. Laos is a bit more laid back than that, but I still didn't want to risk it[1]. However, I'm I'm here to report that it's still pretty damn amusing to watch 35 episodes of *Friends* in a row in what is essentially a clearing in the middle of a Southeast Asian jungle, even if you're not under the influence of mind-altering substances.

Of course, we very nearly missed out on this special cultural experience. On the way to Vang Vieng, as we careened along half-finished roads through the Laotian countryside in a creaking minivan, Liz suggested that we should avoid indulging in the guilty pleasures of the town's TV bars. Her argument was that we ought to spend all of our time exploring the trails, caves and indigenous villages that surround the area.

I wasn't so sure. Right before leaving Luang Prabang I'd come down with a cold, my coughing and snotting making our six hour minivan ride all the more miserable. I was so out of it upon our arrival that I spurned the money-saving idea of splitting a room with a fellow traveler, instead stomping off to find my own digs with Liz in tow. To me, lazing out in front of a TV for the first time in months sounded downright amazing.

With a $3 per night room booked and our heavy bags safely locked away, we were finally able to grab a bit of real food and relax. We were both exhausted from the journey, so it didn't take long to wear down Liz's defenses and drag her across the street to the first TV bar we could find. From the looks of things they were somewhere in the middle of season seven or eight – after Ross and Rachel had a baby out of wedlock, but before Chandler and Monica started getting serious. It wasn't classic *Friends*, but it was a nice, solid run of

---

[1] Neither of us is a recreational drug user anyway. My biggest vices are booze and whatever the stuff is they use to deep-fry McDonald's French Fries.

episodes before the show amped up the sentimentality just before its grand finale. In short, it would do.

One of the weird things about traveling for an extended period in the third world is that it's easy to completely lose your sense of time. Imagine it: You have virtually unlimited money (relative to your expenses) and zero responsibilities. The particular evening I have been describing to you took place in late December, and the only real thing we absolutely *had* to do in life was make it to Bangkok by March for a series of flights to Argentina.

As I sat there watching Joey accidentally propose to Rachel, soothing my raw throat with mango smoothie after mango smoothie, it occurred to me that this was the only thing in the world I needed to accomplish. Truly, the only thing propelling us forward on our trip was our man-made – or rather woman-made – itinerary, an artificial guideline that would have us spend nearly as much time riding buses, trains and boats as not in the next sixty days.

It was tempting to consider the alternative – toss the itinerary; we can do whatever we want! Why visit Vietnam? Liz had already warned me that the country wouldn't be as "easy" to travel in as Thailand or Laos. We could spend another couple weeks in Vang Vieng, pop down to Vientiane for some French food, then circumvent the rest of our loop through Southeast Asia and head back to Thailand for a boatload of beach time.

Right about now, you're probably asking yourself what's wrong with me. No, not what's wrong with you, the reader. What's wrong with *me*, your author and friendly narrator. *Why would this jerk who's lucky enough to get almost an entire year off work want to waste so much time sitting around watching* Friends *in the middle of nowhere?* It's a fair question, considering I haven't revealed Vang Vieng's other main attraction yet.

What if I told you that there was a small river that ran through Vang Vieng? And that this river is mostly slow and shallow, with a few deep spots for diving. In other words, a river perfect for inner tubing. Of course at this point it would be prudent to remind you that it's almost always sunny and extremely hot and humid in Laos, so one would have ideal inner-tubing weather nearly every day. What if I then went on to inform you that dozens of makeshift bamboo bars have sprung up along the riverside? And that some of the bars have set up massive towers equipped with bungee cords, platforms and even zip lines, which travelers can plunge into the water after becoming sufficiently lubricated on the local rice whisky. Would you find this information relevant?

Okay, I concede, it's still not enough to justify more than about a week in the town, but you have to admit that unbelievable natural beauty, drunken inner tubing and endless *Friends* reruns are a seductive combination. I had a great time in Vang Vieng in spite of the Asian Death Bacteria that had infected my sinuses. We hit all the recommended attractions – one day spent riding a rented motorbike through the countryside, swimming in a lagoon, spelunking a cavern, followed by dinner and *Friends*. The next day? Breakfast, *Friends,* drunken inner tubing, *Friends,* dinner, *Friends, Friends,* dessert, *Friends.* The day after that? *Friends, Friends, Friends, Friends,* nap, *Friends, Friends,* internet, *Friends.*

Yep, things were going pretty well for us in Vang Vieng. And you know, I think I just may have been able to persuade Liz to stay a little bit longer if it weren't for another quirky Western hobby the Lao people seem to have become obsessed with: Karaoke.

It's amazing really – the people of Laos have put up with an awful lot over the years, and yet you'd never guess it based on their happy-go-lucky way of life. They're charming in a very sincere way – never in the sort of jaded, sales-y way like some of the Thais who have been dealing with tourists for years. They're entrepreneurial but never pushy like their neighbors in Vietnam. Traveling in Laos is fun, safe and relatively easy[1]. And yet there is one way in which I believe the Lao people have been seriously stunted by the various tragedies that have been perpetrated on them over the years – they have no musical talent.

It's hardly their fault. Until recently, popular music was *not even allowed as an art form* in their country! During the '60s, '70s, '80s and '90s, when the rest of the world – even Vietnam – was experiencing musical growing pains, going from the British invasion to the Disco era to synth rock to hip-hop to Michael Bolton to Color Me Badd to Nirvana to the crowning achievement of all musical theory, Britney Spears, Laos was shut out from it all. They were bombed from all sides, closed off to the rest of the world and largely ignored. When they finally stopped getting bombed and land-mined into oblivion and put together some sort of independence, their new government promptly outlawed pop music. So, is it really a big surprise that they're completely terrible at it?

I hope you don't think that I simply don't enjoy Lao music because it's different. Trust me, by any objective standard, Lao Pop is the worst sort of ear poison you can imagine. By comparison, the amateur Thai kids we saw performing original pop songs (in

---

[1] And getting easier as China continues building and improving roads throughout Laos for its own nefarious purposes.

Thai, mind you) at a Loy Krathong festival sounded like the Beatles on Ed Sullivan.

Lao Pop is whiny, treble-y, reverb-y, quavering, off-key howling like you might find a smashed local belting out in the karaoke bar of a 24-hour bowling alley somewhere on the outskirts of Vegas. And that's just their "produced" music. Degrade it another few notches and you have Lao Karaoke – horrifyingly produced music sung by the most amateur singers imaginable.

You know how at the start of a season of "American Idol" all they do is show terrible singers completely fucking up songs? That's what the music in Laos is like *all the time*. And here's the bad news – they fucking love it! Bless their hearts, they get together in the evenings, down a few shots of Lao Lao, absolutely shit on and destroy the art form of music with their Karaoke singing, then laugh and high five about it until the wee hours of the night. It is a spectacle to behold.

Unfortunately for us, it was a spectacle we could overhear from our $3 hotel room all night long, every night. Technically, the government imposes a curfew in Laos – all restaurants and bars are supposed to close at 11pm. But this was the holiday season and the town was overrun with young travelers who were used to staying up all night on New Year's Eve. On December 31, after a pleasurable day of – what else – *Friends* and inner tubing, Liz and I tossed and turned and groaned our way through a Lao Karaoke-filled night en route to less than three hours of decent sleep.

And just like that, the dream of wasting another week or two lounging around in Vang Vieng died a sudden, violent death. While *Friends* nurtured me back to health in the daytime, the vile, ear-splitting Lao karaoke drained my very life force each and every night. I couldn't live this way any longer, so I agreed it was time to head south for the relatively refined comforts of the "big city" Vientiane.

If you put any stock in the Butterfly Effect[1], it was the perfect time to leave. After all, if we hadn't gone to Vietnam, we wouldn't have seen Ho Chi Minh's body, which means this book would have been one chapter shorter. And if we had made it to the Thai Islands any earlier, we may not have been able to meet up with our friend Austin. Which means that there may not have been a pants-pooping. Which means this book would have been *two* chapters shorter.

---

[1] The idea that small, seemingly insignificant actions can have massive repercussions in the future. Also, an Ashton Kutcher movie.

13. Oops, I Crapped My Pants

If you've read more than about two or three travel books in your lifetime, you had to know this was coming. Apparently it's not a trip to the third world until someone poops their pants, which is just one of the many reasons I was initially opposed to such a trip. Thankfully, a third party did the honors for us this time around, saving Liz and me the indignity of admitting our own incontinence in print.

We were nearing the end of our time in Asia. We'd completed the insane jungle trek in Thailand, gone tubing in Laos and dodged motorbikes up and down Vietnam. All along, we were looking forward to spending our last 30 days in Southeast Asia back in Thailand, hopping from island to island in search of the perfect beach[1].

We also were excited about meeting up with our friend Austin from Bangkok again. He was going to be visiting the Thai islands on assignment – taking photos and researching food for a prominent travel guide. His friend Sarah from the States was also going to be in Thailand, so the four of us agreed to meet up on one of the islands.

One problem: We couldn't agree on an island. Austin needed to do research on Ko Samui, Sarah wanted to go to the Full Moon Party on Ko Pha Ngan, and Liz and I weren't excited about the prospect of either one. See, Ko Samui is one of Thailand's most developed islands. Its most famous beach – Chaweng – could have been lifted straight from Southern California. We wanted something a little quieter. And Ko Pha Ngan? As far as we knew, the Full Moon Parties were the only reason to go there, and neither of us wanted anything to do with them.

---

[1] We found it. See Chapter 14 for details.

It's not that we don't like parties – far from it – but the Full Moon Party is an entirely different beast. Apparently the tradition of throwing a giant rager on Haad Rin Beach every time the moon comes out dates back to the late 70s, when only hard-core travelers and true hippies visited the Thai islands. There were probably a lot of drugs, some groovy music and a mellow time was had by all.

But just like the Thai islands themselves, the Full Moon Party has evolved beyond recognition. Far from a small gathering of backpackers and hippies, the parties are now full-on raves with thumping techno music and tens of thousands of participants. There are definitely a lot of drugs, there's a lot of music (but none of it is groovy), and a mellow time is only had by those people who pass out early in one of the "sleep tents."

Plus, Liz had already been to a Full Moon Party during her first visit to Thailand. Now, eight years older, we had a hard time staying up past midnight. Why should we torture ourselves trying to keep up with 18 year-old ravers who could dance and drink all night without missing a beat?

Our arguments fell on deaf ears. Sarah was going to the party regardless of whether or not anyone else came with her. Austin didn't particularly care about the party, but he wanted to see Sarah, and Ko Samui – the spot he needed to research – was right next to Ko Pha Ngan. It made perfect sense for him to meet her there, then hop the short ferry back to Samui afterward.

So we compromised. Liz and I headed to one of the quieter beaches on Ko Samui, where we intended to spend a few days relaxing while Austin and Sarah went wild on Ko Pha Ngan, then we'd meet up with them after the party. Until a plague of cockroaches changed our plan.

See, in the week or so leading up to the full moon, decent accommodations anywhere on Ko Pha Ngan and even on certain parts of Ko Samui become extremely scarce. Some places jack up their rates and demand a minimum four-night stay – just because they can. Before leaving Ko Phi Phi, we spent hours on the internet trying to book a place. Finally we found one that looked good and had availability, so we called them, only to be told we had to go back online and book from there.

Clouds were gathering as our boat pulled up to Ko Samui, and within five minutes of strapping our bags to the top of a *song tau* it began to rain. The driver kept going for a good five minutes before pulling off the road and covering everyone's bags with a tarp. But it wouldn't matter. We managed to choose a hostel that was 1,000 meters from the main road, and the driver wouldn't take us any closer. Our bags were going to get soaked no matter what.

So we strapped on our already soggy packs and marched through the rain, only to find that the room we thought we had reserved was no longer available. *You never re-confirmed through email*, the American owner said. Well, of course we didn't. Whoever answered the phone had told us to book online – which we did at about 10pm. Our boat then left at 8am the next morning and we were traveling all day... did he expect us to pick up a wireless connection in the middle of the Andaman Sea to check our email?

Regardless of whose fault it was, there was only one room left – a moldy concrete bungalow that felt more like a military barrack than a tropical resort. We told the insincerely apologetic owner we'd think about it, and I sent Liz on an advance scouting mission to find something better along the beach. She wasn't exactly blown away by any of the prospects upon her return, but we both agreed we should avoid giving the first place our business, so off we went.

The "best" places were maybe another thousand meters down the beach, according to Liz. So we stumbled off into the dark, our feet sinking into the wet sand under the weight of backpacks that were getting heavier as they continued absorbing rainwater.

Finally we found a bungalow that seemed good enough. It was a little pricey, but the place was huge and seemed cleaner than most. We paid up, tossed our bags inside and sat down to dinner. Since the owner, maid and cook appeared to all be the same person, we didn't expect much. I ordered a curry, Liz opted for some noodles, and we sat back and waited to be disappointed.

About ten minutes later, the owner/cook/maid brought us one of the best meals we'd had in months. The curry was exquisite and dangerously spicy – far from the bland tourist eats we'd found elsewhere in the islands. And the Beer Chang was honestly the coldest beer I'd ever tasted – the perfect way to wash down a meal so hot it made my eyes water.

We ordered another giant beer, then sat back and reflected. We had good food, cold beer and a roof over our heads. And even though it was raining, we were sitting on a beach in the gulf of Thailand. Life was looking up. After dinner we complimented the owner/cook/waitress/maid/dishwasher on the meal and retired to our bungalow.

We spotted the first roaches simultaneously – I in the bathroom and Liz in the bedroom. *There's a cockroach in here!* we shouted in unison, still disconcerted and upset every time we encountered one of the little bastards in our personal space. Rushing to a safe middle ground, we discussed the situation. The bathroom roach was ominously large, but he appeared content perched on the wall halfway between the sink and the toilet. Both were therefore still usable.

But Liz's roaches were a little more worrisome. She had gone to grab something out of her bag only to send several roaches scattering upon moving it. Conventional wisdom about roaches is that if you find one, you can assume several more are lurking. We had just found half a dozen – we didn't like the way the night was shaping up.

Quickly we decided to throw all our bags on the second bed in the hope that the roaches wouldn't dare advance onto that sacred territory in broad daylight. But, in a move General Custer would have appreciated, a few bold roaches braved the harsh fluorescent light and began exploring the bags right under our noses.

Their gutsy strategy paid off. We could do nothing in the face of such blatant disregard for the normal human/cockroach relationship. They're supposed to lurk in the shadows and we're supposed to smash them with shoes if we ever see them out and about in the daylight.

With these rogue roaches flaunting the rules of engagement, actually digging into the bags to retrieve our protective sleep-sheets was out of the question. The only cockroach-deterrents we had left were a weak overhead fan and an ill-fitting top sheet that almost, but not quite, covered both of us at once. We spent the rest of the night with the lights on, playing tug-of-war with our sweaty top sheet, trying to ignore a particularly loud gecko that sounded as if it were hiding inside the wall behind our bed.[1]

---

[1] We later learned that this was probably a Tokay Gecko, known for their loud "TOH-KAY" croak, their aggressive nature and the fact that they can grow up to a foot long. It's probably for the best that we didn't have access to this information at the time.

When it was bright enough to stop pretending to sleep, we scrambled out of the room and spent the rest of the morning on the beach waiting for our friend Austin. He was going to stop by on his way to Ko Pha Ngan, and we knew without even discussing it that we'd be going with him – we couldn't spend another night in *Joe's Apartment.*

After cautiously gathering our things and checking out, we hopped the ferry and were massively overpaying for a tuk-tuk on Ko Pha Ngan within the hour. Sarah had even managed to reserve a beachside bungalow for us on a day-to-day basis – no small feat during the days leading up to a full moon party.

Exhausted from our night-long battle with the freak mutant roaches on Ko Samui, we had a mellow first night on Pha Ngan. After dinner and a few beers with Austin and Sarah on the beach, we retired early to a room with a protective mosquito net and roaches that actually had the decency to scatter when we flipped the lights.

The next day we set about exploring our new beach. The island of Ko Pha Ngan was a lot bigger than I pictured – our beach (Haad Yao) was about half an hour by tuk-tuk from the dock where we had arrived the day before. And, contrary to the island's reputation, it was actually peaceful. Far from the madness associated with the full moon parties, Haad Yao was a tranquil paradise with white sand beaches and crystal-clear water. It was exactly what we were looking for – in the last place we ever expected to find it. Go ahead, try reading that line in the "movie trailer guy" voice if you like. It's the feel-good hit of the summer!

Invigorated by a night of good sleep and a day spent swimming and sunning in paradise, we discussed our plans for the upcoming full moon party over dinner. It turned out that the original party date – the following night – had been moved due to a conflicting Buddhist holiday. It would have made sense to hold the party the night after the holiday, but there were Thai elections that weekend, which meant it would be forbidden to sell alcohol. Drugs or no drugs, the full moon parties are still mostly fueled by alcohol, so it would have been a major bummer to hold one during a dry weekend. So the party was pushed back yet again, confusing the plans of thousands of young, anxious ravers all across the island who had come to Ko Pha Ngan specifically for the party.

To encapsulate: The island's population was swollen with young party animals who had just found out that the biggest party they would probably ever attend had been pushed back nearly a week. Further, the following night would be their last chance to consume alcohol for nearly 3 days. If that's not a recipe for a pants-pooping, I don't know what is.

The next day – the date of the original full moon party (when the moon was actually full) – we didn't set out to make drunken fools of ourselves up and down Haad Yao Beach. But, these kinds of things are rarely planned. Our drunken spree evolved organically from a simple dinner. One Beer Chang led to another, which led to a discussion about whether we should order something harder, which led to the eventual consumption of four buckets of rum, which led to the stripping off of clothes and running into the ocean.

Technically I don't think you can call it skinny dipping because most of us were too drunk to even bother undressing all the way. But given that I was wearing thin white boxer shorts that went transparent when wet, the difference was nominal. I don't remember paying our mammoth tab at the restaurant, nor do I remember collecting my clothes after we were done swimming, but I do recall that the four of us crashed another group's gathering on the beach, and that I had a 40-minute conversation with a British kid about how he should visit the States because the girls there would dig his accent. This, of course, took place while I was still wearing nothing but a pair of wet, see-through boxers.

Needless to say, it was an epic night. The food, the drink, the nudity – it was the kind of party that only comes around once in a blue moon. Which is probably for the best, because I simply can't handle those kinds of nights very often anymore.

The next morning was about what you'd expect from a group of people who had collectively drunk enough Thai moonshine to stagger Ozzy Osbourne in his prime – we all stumbled out of our respective beds and down the beach to our favorite breakfast spot in a haze, where we laughed and pieced together memories from the previous night over coffee. We were all a little worse for wear, but it was soon apparent that one of us – Sarah – was in a far more serious state than the others.

While we playfully joked about whether or not we actually paid the bill and discussed the varying degrees of our hangovers, she remained stone-faced in her seat, her mouth slack and her eyes boring holes into the salt and pepper shakers in the middle of our table. Her response, when asked if she was all right, was a fey wave of the hand and a whisper of a head nod before returning to her zombielike fixation on our condiments. While the rest of us were regaining our strength, she was fading.

She was progressing through the five stages of an extreme hangover with alarming speed. The zombie trance is stage one. Burying your head in your hands and emitting a persistent low moan is stage two. Sitting on the floor, "just for a little while," is stage three, which Sarah reached in record time. Stage three is usually the point of no return, and, as expected, Sarah moved on to stage four – a sudden, mad rush to the bathroom – post haste.

As she dashed off, we nodded knowingly at one another, having all been there before. But little did we know that Sarah had the final two stages out of order. Before even making it to the bathroom, she blasted through to the rarely achieved stage 5 – Code Brown – literally shitting herself on the way to the can.

With our poor friend trapped helpless in the bathroom with a pair of ruined pants, we chattered on unknowing, probably ordering another round of pancakes and high-fiving each other. It wasn't until ten or fifteen minutes had passed that we realized there may have been complications during stage four, and sent Liz into the contaminated zone for a report.

When the report came back, "new pants are needed," I, for one, was shocked, but also a little proud in a weird sort of way. It was like our night of debauchery had been validated somehow by one of our members paying the ultimate price. Sarah was the party martyr, and we all bowed our heads gravely when she finally emerged from the bathroom.

The whole amazing evening and its unexpected aftereffects, unfortunately, left us in a bit of a pickle. The full moon party was still several days away, giving Sarah time to recover – that wasn't the problem. No, the real issue was that we had set the bar extremely high. Guzzling alcohol from a bucket, skinny dipping, actually shitting ourselves the morning after – these are party feats that cannot, and should not, be topped anytime soon. How could the full moon party be anything but a major disappointment after what we'd just experienced?

With nothing much to do but swim, eat and lie on the beach for the next several days, we pondered the matter. I came full circle to my original line of thinking and decided that we should skip the party altogether, but couldn't persuade anyone else to join me. Sarah was particularly gung-ho about not missing the party. Such a trouper.

When the time finally came, we chartered a *song tau* with several belligerently drunk Italian backpackers and embarked on the treacherous, hilly journey – made even more treacherous by tropical rain – to the other side of the island and the infamous Haad Rin beach.

It was chaos. From the hordes of body-painted backpackers to the western-style fast-food stalls to the 80-million decibel techno that blasted from stacks of busted speakers, it was everything we wanted to avoid in a Thai island, conveniently jammed into a single half-mile crescent.

First order of business: Get drunk enough to make the music tolerable. I'm not some kind of snob that can't appreciate any form of electronic music, but this was the worst of the worst: boring, repetitive "dance music" that amounts to little more than an endless, thumping beat. Give me some old-school hip hop, some remixed pop songs, some turntablists – even some dated Moby or "Fratboy Slim" at the very least. We walked the length of the party – a good half mile or so – in search of tunes more to our liking. Sarah was a self-proclaimed DJ and dance music expert, and she agreed we were hearing C-/D+ level stuff.

So, drinks were in order. But before diving straight into the hard stuff, we figured it would be a good idea to sit down to a meal first and start with a beer. I'm not sure if it was the amount of food we ate, or the pressure of being stone-cold sober in a crazy party environment, but we all noted that even guzzling a round of large, notoriously strong Beer Chang failed to make a dent in our sobriety.

Now dangerously full of food and beer but still feeling like uncool chaperones at a high school dance, we wandered back out into the main party environment – the beach – in search of the ideal bucket. Back on Haad Yao, our "home beach," buckets of alcohol were kind of a novelty. At the full moon party, on the other hand, they're the beverage of choice. Hundreds of rickety bamboo stands advertised everything from "cheap buckets" to "good buckets" – even the boastfully named "fucking good buckets."

Just in case you've been picturing us drinking out of some antique wooden well bucket this whole time, I'll expand my description of the Thai "bucket." Picture a plastic beach bucket – the kind little kids build sandcastles with. Only instead of a little shovel, these buckets come with a 375ml bottle of alcohol – usually Smirnoff vodka, Jack Daniels whisky or Sang Som Thai rum – and a mixer. The mixers range from the usual western soft drinks like Coke and 7-Up to the heart-hammering combination of Red Bull or M-150[1].

We were already dragging, so we ignored our inner cardiologists and went with a Red Bull and Smirnoff bucket. With a different brand of distorted techno blasting from every beachfront bar, conversation was next to impossible, so we simply found an open square of beach and plopped down in the sand to enjoy our bucket and watch other people make fools of themselves.

---

[1] M-150 tastes just like Red Bull, but it has a more impressive slogan emblazoned on its label: "Devotion, Courage, Sacrifice." It's not just an energy drink; it's a way of life.

At any given full moon party, there could be anywhere from 10 to 20,000 participants. But you'll rarely find a single person among them doing anything other than the following five activities:

1. Drinking
2. Dancing
3. Doing Drugs
4. Trying to light themselves on fire
5. Peeing into the Ocean

Let me elaborate. The three D's are pretty standard party behavior around the world, but there's something special about the full moon party that incites otherwise normal partygoers to attempt to engulf themselves in flames by participating in activities such as flaming jump rope, flaming obstacle course and flaming limbo. We also witnessed a kind of flaming Red Rover game, in which people line up on either side of a series of flaming lines on the beach, then take turns rushing across to the other side. We saw one massive frat boy take off at the same time as a petite blond on the other side – he unknowingly pancake blocked her into the fire and was off high-fiving his friends while she lay writhing in a pit of fiery death[1]. Good times.

As for peeing into the ocean, I'm here to report that it's strangely liberating. When else is it socially acceptable to pee in front of 20,000 strangers? Imagine it... you wander out into the surf, unzip, take a look

---

[1] Despite the high volume of alcohol that was almost certainly coursing through her veins, she did not spontaneously combust but rather was able to recover without serious injury and even take another run.

around and notice that about 40 other guys are doing the exact same thing at perfectly spaced intervals along the entire beach. Then you take a deep breath of fresh ocean air and let 'er rip without a care in the world. Is urine washing up around your ankles? Almost certainly. But surely this is a small price to pay for such an invigorating and organic bathroom experience. Never are you more at one with nature than when you are pissing directly into it.

As much fun as it was to pee into the ocean and watch people light themselves on fire, we weren't getting any drunker and the music was still terrible. We kept ordering more buckets, more beer – trying in vain to recreate the magic of our earlier soiree. But it was a lost cause. We finally ended up dancing a little bit and I could see how it would be easy to be swept away by the energy of the crowd even if the music wasn't to your liking.

At half past two in the morning we took a break and headed to the strip of fast-food joints just inland of the beach. The idea was that we'd just take a quick pit-stop – a chance to refuel with a little greasy food before heading back out there and partying all night long. But after our stomachs were laden with a couple rounds of weinerschnitzel and French fries, we found that our hearts just weren't in it. We grabbed a taxi and retreated to our side of the island, having lasted less than half the night.

I think of all of us, Sarah was the most disappointed. She'd been expecting great dance music and a wild drunken time that lasted all night long. Instead we found ourselves back at our home beach – which was as quiet as a Buddhist temple that night – at a somewhat reasonable hour. She had to catch a flight the next day and was on a boat before the rest of us even woke up. But hey, at least she pooped her pants. That's a memory that will last a lifetime.

14. "The" Beach

Although we split our time in Southeast Asia between four countries, we spent a total of three and a half months in the region – more than any place else on our trip. And while Thailand, Laos, Vietnam and Cambodia each have their own distinct flavor, there are enough similarities between the four to make you feel like the whole place is one big, crowded country. That is, if you're able to purge all recollection of the annoying border crossings from your memory.

Still, there are a few spots in each country that are truly unique. Like Angkor Wat in Cambodia. Hanoi in Vietnam. Vang Vieng in Laos. And, of course, "The Beach" in Thailand. Surely you know which "The Beach" I'm referring to. For better or worse, when the average American thinks of Thailand, they picture a shirtless Leonardo DiCaprio diving off a waterfall in *The Beach*, the 2000 movie based on Alex Garland's novel of the same name.

True story: When I first watched the movie – particularly the scenes where Leo wanders up and down Khao San road and, later, visits a sleazy looking bar on Ko Pha Ngan – I made a mental note never to visit Thailand. The place looked so out of control and wild; I was certain I would hate it. Ten years later, having visited most of the places Leo did, I can confirm that the movie (and the book, which is a fair bit better than the movie) captured Khao San Road and Ko Pha Ngan *perfectly*. And yet, I loved Khao San road, I loved Ko Pha Ngan and I loved Thailand overall. In retrospect, perhaps I shouldn't have based my travel philosophy so heavily on a Leonardo DiCaprio movie. (Although I still think we can all learn several important lessons from *Titanic).*

In any case, when it came time to decide which Thai islands to visit,[1] Liz and I got into a classic travel argument. It goes something like this: Given a choice, Liz always wants to visit the less popular spots. The further off the beaten path, the better. I, on the other hand, tend to think that the more popular spots have become that way for a reason, and that it's worth putting up with the crowds and the development to check them out.

She won the first round of this ongoing battle and Ko Mak was the first Thai Island we visited together. Nearby Ko Chang is much more popular and known for its stunning white beaches and electric blue water. But Liz suspected that it had been "ruined" by a plague of tourists and the accompanying development to meet their demands.

So, Ko Mak it was. Pulling up in a speedboat, our first impressions were good – the water was shockingly green, the beaches seemed wide and uncluttered by development and, best of all, we didn't meet a single hotel tout on the pier. It was quiet and peaceful, and we found a cute little bungalow just a stone's throw from the water.

But upon further exploration, the beaches were a little bit rocky after all. And the water was kind of choppy and not nearly as pretty as it had looked zipping by at 370 miles per hour on the boat. Worst of all, there was kind of a lot of garbage strewn about. Don't get me wrong; the place was still darn close to paradise. But relative to all the other incredible beaches we would eventually see during the course of our trip, I'd give Ko Mak about a C-minus.

The next island we visited was also a Liz pick. Ko Lanta, over in the Andaman Sea, was a little more

---

[1] There are hundreds of islands, and dozens with significant development.

developed than Ko Mak, but cleaner and brighter, with some of the nicest water we'd ever seen. A solid B+.

After Ko Lanta, we had some tougher decisions to make. Our original plan was to visit Railay Beach, which another group of travelers had described as "life-changing." On paper it was a slam dunk – it was one of the first places we completely agreed on. But the more we read about the place, the less appealing it sounded. Although Railay isn't actually an island, you can only reach it by boat. But it's not a long enough boat ride to necessitate the use of large ferries. Consequently there are supposedly a million smaller longtail boats clogging up the bay, polluting the air and water with their outboard motors and damaging precious coral reefs with carelessly tossed anchors.

Suddenly Railay sounded like Liz's worst nightmare and I saw an opening. I'd wanted to visit Ko Phi Phi since I read in our Lonely Planet that that was where they'd filmed all the spectacular beach scenes in *The Beach*. You remember that part – shortly after Leo finds the secret utopian society, he walks down to visit their private beach as the camera pans a magnificent cliff-ringed bay with crystal-clear water and white sand.

I pulled up a screenshot of that precise scene on our laptop, pointed at it and said simply, "I want to go there." Liz shrugged.

"It's not going to look like that," she said. "Everyone says 'The Beach' is developed beyond recognition. It's supposedly crowded and dirty and I heard they even put an ugly concrete pier in the water. Think about how many people went there after the movie came out."

She had a point, but I wasn't giving up that easily. "Yeah, well unless they put a few hotels directly on top of those fucking cliffs, I'm guessing the view hasn't changed," I said. "I don't care how crowded the beach is, I don't care how many hotels they've built, I

don't even care if the only view I can get is from the
Starbucks stand in the McDonald's parking lot; I want
to see those cliffs! We're fucking going!"

My out-of-the-blue passion and anger won the
day, and it wasn't long before we were approaching the
crescent-shaped bay of Ko Phi Phi Don. From our
viewpoint atop the ferry, it didn't look good at first. The
water was nice, but there *was* an unfortunate concrete
pier stapled onto the side of the island, and lots of ugly
boats cluttering up the view. I began to panic. It didn't
even look like any of the beaches were usable, let alone
the kind of pristine spots I'd promised Liz we'd find.

I double checked Lonely Planet to make sure we
had the right island, and discovered to my relief that
the other side of Ko Phi Phi Don is the one that's
supposed to be nice. After disembarking and fighting
our way through a phalanx of touts, we wandered
through the island's dense maze of restaurants, hotels,
bars and shops before finally popping out into the clear
on the other side. Before settling on a hotel, we walked
the long, uneven path to the beach – to make sure we'd
be near a good spot.

It was nice, but not quite as nice as in the
movie. There were a few cliffs, sure, but somehow in
the film they looked bigger and better. And yeah, it was
crowded, and the beach was packed with umbrellas and
chairs that you had to rent if you wanted a place to sit.
Pretty much the kind of place Liz had wanted to avoid.
So that's it, huh, we said in unison, before trudging
back into the thick of the developed area and
overpaying for a cramped, stuffy room.

Now if this story were, in fact, a movie, I think it
would be a lot closer to *National Lampoon's Vacation*
than *The Beach*, and this would be the part where a
frazzled Clark Griswold and his family arrive at Wally
World after weeks of arduous travel, only to find that
the park is closed for repairs. Because it turns out that

The Beach wasn't filmed on Ko Phi Phi Don at all... it was filmed on Ko Phi Phi *Leh!*

Boy was my face red. All the haggling and negotiating I had to go through just to visit the set of *The Beach,* and we didn't even land on the right freaking island. But not all was lost. It turned out that Ko Phi Phi Leh was less than half an hour from Ko Phi Phi Don (thank God) and that "The Beach" was actually Maya Bay, a fact that I soon confirmed through a closer examination of our Lonely Planet guidebook.

So, what were we waiting for? My first thought was to re-pack our bags and scoot on over to *Leh* as soon as possible. It wasn't that simple. It turned out that Ko Phi Phi Leh was a national park of sorts. And while that designation hasn't necessarily prevented other Thai locations from being exploited and/or ruined by unscrupulous developers, for some reason, it has protected Ko Phi Phi Leh. There is *no* development on the island. Not a single hotel, guest house or restaurant. A solitary public restroom is the only amenity.

Bad news for my plan to stay on the island, perhaps, but great news for the preservation of one of the world's best beaches. That cliff-ringed paradise from *The Beach?* It actually did exist, and we were going to get to see it in its virgin state.

First things first, we had to book a tour to Maya Bay, which wasn't as easy as it seemingly should have been. I mean sure, there were a million local tour offices that advertised an afternoon on *The Beach,* but every tour I could find also included a bunch of other activities and locations that I had no interest in – like snorkeling, spelunking and a visit to "Monkey Island."

I know I'm in the minority here, but I can't stand monkeys. Their cute faces and furry little bodies belie their aggressive, biting nature. Sure, those little fuckers look innocent, but they're strong enough to rip your arms off and beat you to death with them, if they were so inclined. So, thanks but no thanks, I'll pass on Monkey Island.

The only problem was that it was looking more and more like Monkey Island and Maya Bay were a package deal. There wasn't a single tour agency on Ko Phi Phi Don that offered a direct day-trip to Maya Bay and Maya Bay only. They all included snorkeling, spelunking and goddamned Monkey Island. Finally I figured out why: Despite the multitudes of travel agencies, all with their own posters and signs advertising the trips, there were only *two* actual tour companies that visited Maya Bay.

The first was the company that offered the Monkey Island package, which only allowed for about an hour in Maya Bay. *Don't you want to see Monkey Island and go snorkeling too?* the travel agents asked, incredulous that I would pass up a chance to visit an island populated with evil, vicious, foul-smelling little beasts.

The second tour company offered a chance to "Spend the Night on *The Beach!*" No mucking around with Monkey Island; this tour went directly to Maya Bay, where we'd be allowed to play a quick game of soccer, scarf down some rice and curry, then pitch tents and bunk down for the night. I was intrigued, until I found out it cost four times as much as the other tour and you didn't get to spend any daylight hours at Maya Bay. Rather, you arrived at dusk and left first thing in the morning. Brilliant. You don't suppose anyone would want to actually spend the sunny part of the day on the best beach in the world, do you?

Fed up with the lack of choices, I tried to charter my own boat. Talking to a couple guys down at the pier, I found that we could get three hours in a longtail boat for about 2,000 baht (~$60 USD). However, that didn't include a 500-baht "park fee" *per person* that was supposedly included in all the package tours. Given that we'd spend one of our three hours just traveling to and fro, it didn't seem worth the extra cash just to buy one additional hour on the beach.

Discouraged, I finally gave up. There's just no way to spend any significant amount of time at *The Beach* unless you're willing to spend well over $100, or you have your own boat. Fuming with rage, I went back to one of the Monkey Island travel agencies, slammed my baht down on the desk and told them I'd take it.

Our trip began in predictable fashion. The tour guide, a scrawny Thai teenager who appeared to be affecting a Johnny Depp in *Pirates of the Caribbean* look, scratchily informed us that he had had too much to drink the night before, and had lost his voice. Ah well, no big deal. It's not as though his job is to verbally guide people on a tour. Oh wait.

And we got off to a late start, which, our guide solemnly informed us, meant that we would have to skip Monkey Island. Now wait just a minute. I wasted all that time trying to avoid stupid Monkey Island, only to be told that it wasn't possible, and there we were skipping it anyway. I still had absolutely zero interest in visiting Monkey Island, mind you, but now I felt cheated!

The next stop was the Viking Cave, a tiny crack in the side of one of Phi Phi Leh's cliffs, which is filled with valuable swiftlet bird's nests. Armed guards oversee a group of harvesters who must climb precarious bamboo scaffolds to obtain the nests. Primo "first nests" are worth well over $1,000 a pound, and are used in everything from indigenous medicine to soup to a particularly disturbing beverage distributed in the United States by Wonderfarm[1].

---

[1] Bird's Nest or "White Fungus" drink – dare your friends and family to try it! Available in most Asian markets.

Hmm, armed guards, thousand-dollar bird's nests and a bunch of dudes scrambling up tenuously held-together scaffolding – this actually sounded interesting. But did we get to go inside the cave? No. Did we get to pull up right next to the cave so we could at least see inside? No. Did we simply breeze past the cave from a distance of about 400 meters while our tour guide rattled off a bunch of gibberish in a hoarse whisper? Yes. Yes we did.

At this point I threw up my hands, looked over at Liz with a reluctant smile and admitted that she was right all along. We shouldn't have come to this overdeveloped group of Thai Islands. And I should have known that this tour was bound to disappoint, as it tried to pack six activities into just three hours. Still, we had three stops left, and having skipped Monkey Island and blitzed past Viking Cave without so much as slowing down, at least we were actually back on schedule.

That meant a full 40 minutes for the next activity, snorkeling. Now, Liz has her open water SCUBA certificate, so snorkeling to her is kind of like driving a go-kart directly after putting the pedal to the metal in a Ferrari. I hadn't been scuba diving, but I had done some mediocre snorkeling in Cambodia the previous week, so my expectations weren't particularly high either.

But, much to our surprise, we had a great time. The visibility was excellent and we were able to see hundreds of exotic fish and even some coral reef. We spent the full allotted time paddling around excitedly, and by the time we clambered back onto the boat, exhausted, we agreed that this single activity had been worth the price of admission.

Ah, but we still hadn't seen *The Beach*. It was the next stop, Jack Sparrow informed us, and we'd have just under an hour to spend once we got there. Rounding the island, we reached the entrance to Maya Bay and offloaded into a handful of smaller boats for the final leg of the trip. The water was already kind of a magical green color, and it simply became brighter and more intense as we approached the shore.

Here's the part where I turn into a stereotypical travel writer and begin gushing uncontrollably. Maya Bay is fucking amazing. It is, without a doubt, the best beach I've ever visited. The sand alone is enough reason to visit – it's perfect. It's the lightest, most feathery soft white sand you'll ever set foot on. There are no rocks, no shells, no driftwood or human pollution fouling things up; just perfect, unspoiled white sand.

And the water. The water is remarkably calm and the perfect depth and temperature for lounging. Overall, it's shallow, so you can walk way out and admire the cliffs from a different perspective. But there's enough depth to practice your freestyle stroke, too. And if you explore the edges of the bay near the cliffs, there are supposed to be a few great spots for snorkeling.

We didn't bother checking them out. We spent the whole hour just gaping at the spectacular view, then taking turns rolling around in the sand before running and jumping into the water, giggling like a couple of drunken rednecks on a cow-tipping spree the entire time.

It was so spectacular that I would have gladly suffered through Monkey Island or even guzzled an entire pint of Bird's Nest drink just to spend an hour on its shore. Sure, more time would have been nice, but as it turned out, an hour was enough. As Jemaine reminds us, *two minutes in heaven is better than one minute in heaven.*

The only way in which Maya Bay didn't live up to my vision of *The Beach* was that it turned out to not be entirely ringed with cliffs like it is in the movie. In real life, there's a small gap which serves as the bay's most convenient entrance. The movie guys just added another cliff in post-production to make the setting jibe with the one in Alex Garland's book.

When our time was up, we reluctantly boarded the longtail boats and ferried back to our larger vessel for the final stop on our tour – sunset watching. This consisted of nothing more than parking the boat parallel with the horizon so we could watch the sun go down, something I might have grumbled about not really being an "activity" under other circumstances, but which I truly enjoyed at that moment in time – having just visited the most glorious beach in the world.

Of course, the surprising enjoyment of our little daytrip left us with a bit of a dilemma: Did Liz get credit for predicting that Ko Phi Phi would be overdeveloped and crowded – as Ko Phi Phi Don most certainly was – or did I get credit for delivering a stunning, unspoiled beach in a destination that snobby, elite travelers dismiss as ruined?

I think the lesson we learned was simply that popularity and awesomeness are not mutually exclusive. On the flip side, for every hidden gem you find going off the beaten path, there are an equal number of lumps of coal that have remained unpopular for a reason. No matter how many guidebooks you read, you never know until you see it for yourself.

So, as a public service to other Reluctant Travelers out there who prefer to go the safe and easy route, the following is a list of attractions on the tourist trail that have managed to retain their original charm. You can have a great time at just about any Thai beach. Angkor Wat is still worth seeing despite the armies of tourists blocking most of the bas-reliefs. The Yucatan Peninsula is still worth a visit despite the fact that it costs people from Florida and Texas less than $100 one-way to get there. And most of the most popular tourist country we visited on our trip – Italy – should still be right at the top of your must-see list. Well, with one notable exception.

15. The Italian Snob

Quick, what's the most romantic city in the world? I'll bet you ten dollars your brain just shouted *Paris!* or *Venice!* Because the unconditional love for both cities in film, music and the rest of pop culture is unparalleled. Have you ever seen a film in which either city is made to look ugly or unpleasant, or heard a song in which either city is anything but romanticized? I sure haven't. And yet I'm here to report that at least one of the *top two* most beautiful, romantic, idealized cities in the world is a completely overblown fraud. Here's a hint: It ain't Paris.

It has probably become evident by this point that our quick pit-stop in Venice was a total trainwreck. Actually, a literal trainwreck might have been preferable to the events as they unfolded. Then we could have calmly stepped from the smoldering ruins of our *Trenitalia* carriage, wandered off into the countryside and probably spent the rest of our days picking olives in ignorant bliss.

Unfortunately, our train arrived safely in Treviso, a medium-sized town that serves as a popular base from which to explore Venice. So, we simply disembarked and waited for our ride, completely unprepared for the misery we were about to experience.

I would now like to issue an official heads-up to any of my Italian relatives reading this book. I am about to throw one of our family friends under the bus. It's nothing personal; I just think this story needs to be told and I've decided that my relationship with this particular person, let's call her Madonna, isn't worth preserving.

Let's back up for a moment. One of my favorite memories from my first trip to Italy was our visit to

Treviso. We stayed with Madonna's family in what I incorrectly remembered as a thousand-year old house on a picturesque orchard[1]. My brother and I watched *The Three Amigos* with their kids, I rode a motorbike for the first time and I debated the merits of American versus Italian pizza with Madonna's husband, Mario. It was awesome.

Sixteen years later, as Liz and I planned our round-the-world adventure, I really hyped up Treviso as a key destination. I gushed about Madonna's hospitality and the idyllic setting of her home. I raved about Venice and how much fun it was to explore the city's narrow, crumbling walkways and bridges. I even secretly dreamed that we would arrive to find Mario polishing a garageful of red Ducatis, which he would then cheerfully offer up for us to borrow any time we liked.

The funny thing is, if Mario did possess a garageful of red Ducatis, I believe he actually *would* have offered to let us borrow one of them. My memories of him as a warm and genuinely friendly guy were accurate. And the kids with whom we watched *The Three Amigos*? We saw them once again as well, and they were both exceedingly friendly, if a little shy. What we had left were Madonna and the city of Venice itself, both of which were awful to very awful.

The first thing you need to know about Madonna is that she grew up in America. She's actually from Portland. She does have an Italian background, like me, but she spent roughly the first half of her life in the United States. I don't have all the exact details, but at some point she did move to Italy, marry an Italian man and raise two Italian children. She has been living

---

[1] There is a small orchard and it is picturesque. But the house is nowhere near a thousand years old. I have no idea where that memory came from.

over there for a significant amount of time. And she has adopted the language, the style and 500% of the attitude.

See, Madonna is a giant snob. She's wealthy (her husband is in medicine and she's a successful businesswoman), and she constantly reminds you of this fact with snide little comments about the city being overrun with beggars or musings about some of the wildly expensive things she'd like to buy while window shopping. In a way, she is the personification of a WASPy rumination taken to the extreme – an American ex-pat who sneers and looks down her nose at anything from her homeland.

Without knowing any of this, I got in touch with my aunt about a month before our trip and asked her to contact Madonna. We were going to be passing through Italy; would it be all right for us to stay a few nights while we explored Venice? Madonna agreed, and we penciled in Treviso as one of the featured stops on our circuit.

Fast-forward to our actual arrival. After almost two weeks living la dolce vita in a Mediterranean villa we'd finally started *traveling,* popping up to Switzerland, back into the Italian alps, through Verona, down to a small town near Parma and eventually to Treviso. We hadn't gotten used to the constantly-on-the-move backpacker lifestyle yet – we were hungry, tired and unwashed – and we had all of our bags with us. The first thing we wanted to do was simply head to Madonna's place and wash up. The *last* thing we wanted to do was take a walking and shopping tour of Treviso followed by an aperitif at a fancy outdoor bar. And yet that is exactly what Madonna forced us to do straight off the train.

Ignoring our hints about the situation, she proceeded to take us on a whirlwind tour of Treviso, stopping every so often at a department store to ogle designer handbags. We could not have had less interest in shopping – we didn't have extra money to spend or any space to carry new purchases around – but that didn't stop Madonna. We smelled and looked terrible; we were in no condition to sit down and sample a "spritz[1]" alongside the well-heeled locals, but Madonna didn't notice or care. One of us could have been bleeding from the head and I think she still would have insisted on showing us the United Colors of Benetton store.

After the exhausting, fast-paced tour, we finally, mercifully, returned to Madonna and Mario's house for dinner. Her daughter had made a fine mushroom risotto, which Madonna criticized before ladling onto our plates. After dishing me up a solid portion, she proceeded to spoon about half as much onto Liz's plate, snorting, "women should eat less than men," without a trace of irony or humor in her tone.

Um, what? I suppose if Liz were overweight, this comment, while spectacularly rude, would have at least made some sense. But Liz is as skinny as a beanpole and runs about nine miles a day. She can certainly eat whatever she wants without having to count calories. Hell, she's a lot skinnier than Madonna[2]! So what gives? It was the first time, but not the last time, that we witnessed pure, unmitigated, nonsensical rudeness for the sake of rudeness coming out of her mouth.

Over dinner Madonna had plenty of further opportunities to make subtle digs at the American way of life, and she made the most of them. Her daughter

---

[1] The signature drink of the region – a cocktail made with white wine, fizzy water and human bile, which is available in bottles labeled "Campari."

[2] The family friend, not the singer with the pointy bra. She's about equally skinny as the singer.

worked for a grocery chain that had hired a team of British and American consultants to streamline and improve their business. Madonna had beef with this. *Their ideas will never work here – they don't understand that we're different. Their "Anglo-Saxon[1]" way of thinking will never fly in Italy – just you watch!*

Without needing to consult one another, at this point Liz and I both knew that we would rather *not* have Madonna accompany us on our trip to Venice the following day, as she had offered to do. But, like any well-trained salesperson or Jehovah's Witness, she would not take no for an answer. We did everything we could to get the message across that we'd rather go alone – without being rude, of course. No dice. She was coming whether we liked it or not.

Having accepted this reality, we started to plan our day. Liz had read in a guidebook that the best time to explore Venice was as early in the morning as possible, when the light would be good for photography and before the daily rush of tourists arrived to clog all the bridges and plazas. Madonna scoffed at this idea. *That's just typical guidebook nonsense; we'll go at 11.*

By the time we were able to finally drag her down to the train station the next morning, many of the scheduled trains had been cancelled[2]. So when a Venice-bound train finally arrived, there were far too many passengers and we had to muscle our way through the crowd just to get on board. Madonna dove into a seat and crossed her arms smugly as Liz and I whirled and danced to find seats of our own before the

---

[1] This word positively dripped with venom as spoken by our lovely hostess. Again, *you're from Portland, bitch!*
[2] For no reason, as far as I could tell. Hey, it turned out that Madonna and I did have one thing in common – we both loved to complain about *Trenitalia*.

entire carriage was filled to standing room only. *You can't be polite,* she knowingly informed us once the train had started rolling. *You have to just shove your way through. Don't let people get in your way.* Good to know.

Once we arrived and managed to distance ourselves ever so slightly from the tidal wave of tourists pouring into the city, Madonna gave us a sharp look. *I told myself I wasn't going to bring visitors to Venice anymore,* she said. Liz and I stole a quick glance at each other in disbelief before she continued. *The last time I brought people here, it took us three hours just to make it to St. Mark's – they wanted to go into every shop!* Once again we told her, as clearly as we knew how, that we had absolutely zero interest in shopping.

Seemingly in agreement that we would blitz through the gauntlet of shops, restaurants and assorted tourist traps en route to St. Mark's plaza and the main architectural wonders of Venice, we skipped down the front steps of the train station and out into one of the clearest, sunniest November days I'd ever experienced. It would have been the perfect day to explore Venice on foot – if it weren't for the fact that approximately 8.3 million other people had the same idea. We found out later that it was an Italian holiday weekend, so in addition to all the foreign tourists, we were getting a crush of Italian ones too.

Still, brightened by the picture-perfect weather, the three of us soldiered on – to the first Venetian mask store. *Oh, let's just stop in for a minute,* Madonna said, so we obliged. I mean, I wasn't about to drop 300 Euros on a delicate, handcrafted mask that probably wouldn't have survived the rest of our time in Italy, let alone the next nine months, but what could I do? Liz and I both smiled and nodded politely as Madonna explained how the masks were a Venetian specialty.

Finally we moved on – to another shop less than 50 feet down the road. This time, Madonna explained all the miniature glass figurines and how they were produced on a nearby island. Another half a block, another shop. At this point I began to question the woman's sanity. She had literally *just told us* that she didn't want to waste three hours stopping in every goddamn shop, and yet that's exactly what she was forcing us to do.

Eventually she dragged us into something moderately cool – an *osteria*, which is a type of small bar that's typical of the region. Generally they serve a wide selection of antipasti which people eat while standing up and guzzling a spritz. Madonna ordered us glasses of white wine, some calamari and a few other appetizers. It was the peak of her hospitality, and probably the best thing we did in Venice. But the good times didn't last long.

Perhaps an hour later we *still* hadn't reached St. Mark's and we were all getting hungry again. Madonna picked out another *osteria* and we ducked inside for a quick bite. This time I told her it was on me, and asked her to pick out a good selection of stuff for us. *If you say so,* she said sarcastically while making a poop-face. Translation: *Sure, buddy, if you think your broke ass can afford this fancy Italian nosh.*

Liz and I nabbed a couple of stools and exchanged meaningful eye-rolls and facial tics while Madonna bullied her way to the front of the bar. *What do you want to drink?* she suddenly shouted at us. I looked around and shrugged. Most people seemed to be drinking red wine. So, um, red wine, I guess? Her response shattered the world record for the most sarcastic tone of voice ever achieved by a human. Tilting her head downward and her eyes dramatically up, she simply said, *Red wine? Oooooookaaaaaay....*

before turning around and ordering 3 glasses of red wine.

I didn't get it. Why did she have to talk like that? Everyone else was drinking red wine, what the fuck was wrong with ordering red wine? There it was again – Madonna was being rude just for the sake of being rude. Just for the sheer "fuck you" of it. That was it. I'd had enough. Annoyance layered upon annoyance was slowly building to anger. What was I going to do about it? Tell her off? Make a scene? "Hulk out" and rip my shirt off in a whirlwind of fury? No, this would be even better. I'll tell you what I was going to do about it. I was only going to speak to Madonna in clipped tones for the rest of our time in Venice and Treviso. That ought to show her.

For the record, I am not listing each and every instance of Madonna's rudeness and odd behavior. Such a compilation would bloat this chapter out of proportion with the rest of the book to such a degree that the entire project would require a new title. Something along the lines of *10,000 Things I Hate About You*. Instead, I will just give you the Cliffs Notes. In addition to the atrocities already listed, Madonna littered blatantly and frequently, stated unilaterally that she "hates Arabs," and claimed that the little old Ukranian ladies out begging on the streets were imported and well-paid by some kind of powerful panhandling syndicate.

All right, enough bitching. A mere two and a half hours after disembarking from our train, we reached St. Mark's square. Without any more shopping in sight, Madonna excused herself and headed back to Treviso. We finally had the rest of the afternoon to ourselves. After venting a bit and shaking our heads in disbelief, we set out to explore what Venice had to offer besides those goddamn masks.

Now, I'm pretty sure that Italy has always been a popular tourist destination, but I remembered Venice being peaceful and relatively empty. Maybe it was an off day when I visited sixteen years earlier, or maybe my memory was flat-out wrong (I did, after all, remember having a great time at Madonna's house), but this was a whole new Venice. Everything was mobbed. The quaint little alleys and bridges? Filled with chattering tourists. St. Mark's Plaza? Teeming with people and pigeons. Even the church was packed to the rafters, with a line that stretched hundreds of meters from the entrance. They say Venice is sinking and I believe it – the sheer weight of all those tourists has got to be putting a massive strain on its ancient foundations.

Plus, the whole city reeked of foul, stagnant water and there was no place to go to the bathroom, unless you wanted to drop some serious Euros in one of the many overpriced cafes. Here's a tip – if you do find yourself in need of the loo, don't sit down at a café. Order your drink standing up if you want to save money. We paid around 8 Euros ($12 at the time) for a small bottled water and a small glass of house wine *from a box* because we made the mistake of sitting down first. The cashier even gave me a "gotcha" smile when my eyes bugged out at the bill.

The crowds, the prices, the smells – these were things that we probably could have overlooked under ordinary circumstances. But after putting up with Madonna's bullshit all morning long, we were spent. We trudged listlessly around and tried to enjoy ourselves until it got dark, when we conceded defeat and headed back to the train station. It was our least favorite city in Italy by a wide margin. Still, it could have been worse. At least the story didn't end with vomit shooting out of my face at 100 miles per hour.

16. Montezuma's Pre-Emptive Strike

One of the genetic traits I inherited from my father is the ability to refrain from vomiting when I have ingested something disgusting. To be clear, this does not include most forms of alcohol (which are obviously delicious, not disgusting). Amazingly, my father has vomited only twice over the course of his 56 years. Once, when he had the flu at age 11. The second time in college, after guzzling too much beer and playing Frisbee with his friends. That's it. The man simply doesn't get sick.

Growing up, it didn't appear that I had inherited his super-stomach gene. I puked plenty of times just like any other kid. Then, on the first day of fourth grade, I got the stomach flu for the last time. From that point on, I never broke a fever. On occasion I'd become nauseous or get an upset stomach, but these rare instances never culminated in actual sickness.

In college I more than one-upped his single binge-drinking overindulgence, but still I remained fever free. I never even got food poisoning, probably thanks to my revolutionary grilled cheese sandwich and Gatorade diet. And in the nearly ten years since then, my streak remained intact. No puking unless I've had too many Long Island Ice teas, no food poisoning and no fever. Ever.

If at this point you're wondering why stories about puking and shitting make up a disproportionate amount of the content in this book, allow me to explain: International traveling contains a disproportionate amount of puking and shitting. I'm just telling it like it is.

I guess in retrospect it's actually surprising – shocking, even – that it took as long as it did for either of us to become violently ill. We'd already been traveling for 240 days, subjecting our stomachs to all kinds of questionable cuisine. By the time we reached Mexico, I figured that if we hadn't gotten sick already, we were probably in the clear. But Mexico has the reputation. You go to Mexico, you get sick. Or so everyone with whom I've ever spoken about the country has told me.

Still, I was confident. We'd been in the country three weeks already. I went on a taco-eating rampage (I literally ate 19 tacos over the course of my first two days in Mexico) with no ill effects. I kept dishing out the punishment and my stomach kept right on taking it like Rocky Balboa. Spicy chorizo sausage? *You ain't so bad!* Greasy tacos by the fistful? *He is like a rock, I cannot break him.* Pure, liquefied habañero peppers? *Yo, Adrienne!*

Plus, we were nearing the end of our travels. In just two days, we'd be in Oaxaca for six weeks. No more lengthy bus rides or filthy hostel bathrooms. No more hours spent lugging our bags around in the hot sun. In other words, no more of the stressful travel conditions that can easily disrupt the fragile ecosystem of one's digestive tract.

Well, it should be obvious that I didn't make it. But before getting into all the glorious details, the story requires some fleshing out. We were in a town called San Cristobal de las Casas, up in the central Mexican highlands. When the Spanish invaders came over and started dominating the Mayans in the Yucatan peninsula back in the 16th century, the area surrounding modern San Cristobal is where many of the survivors fled.

To this day, a large indigenous population remains. And Chiapas State is also one of the strongholds of the Zapatista rebels, an anti-government group that supports indigenous rights. But you'd never know it unless you left the city. The town itself is progressive and hip, with great international restaurants, trendy shopping spots, wine bars and a brisk tourist industry.

Naturally, I didn't want to leave the city to visit the indigenous people or the Zapatista rebels. Why would I? Didn't I just mention the great international restaurants, trendy shopping spots and wine bars? But no. Any time our traveling became too easy, Liz found a way to make it more complicated. Of course we couldn't spend all our time in San Cristobal just hanging out. We needed to cram ourselves into a creaky *colectivo*[1] and ride up into the hills, to a town called San Juan Chamula.

The town is largely made up of indigenous folk, and most well known for its church. There's nothing particularly special about the church itself – it's just an old Catholic church. But what is interesting is that at some point the locals gave Christianity the boot and decided to use the church to worship according to their own unique blend of traditional Mayan and Judeo-Christian beliefs. They've removed the pews, the crosses and most of the Christian decorations from their church, leaving only the statues of the saints, which they've arranged in two rows that span the length of the nave.

Here's where it gets weird. Every day, they spread what appear to be pine needles all over the floor. Then the worshippers enter, clear a little space in front of their favorite saint and light a bunch of candles – often as many as a hundred. They kneel and bow in prayer, sometimes speaking rapidly under their breath, or out loud in a droning monotone, until all the candles have burnt out. And then they take sips from the little glasses of Coke or Sprite or Mirinda they've arranged

---

[1] Spanish for "1989 EuroVan with busted shocks."

next to the candles, hoping to burp out their evil spirits and thereby purify their bodies.

It is quite a scene. I'm not a religious person, so many religious rituals seem a little strange to me. But watching hundreds of people chugging Coke and trying to burp in a dark, smoky church is right up there with anything I'd ever witnessed.

Obviously, the use of modern soft drinks like Coke is a recent addition to the native religion. They've always believed that burping is healthy because it expels negative spirits, but until the advent of carbonated beverages they had to drink massive quantities of water to achieve the same effect.

It's not their only strange belief. A few days prior, Liz and I visited a museum of Mayan medicine and watched a video on traditional childbirth. The village midwife is shown waving a live rooster around the body of the mother and rubbing her with eggs. After the mother gives birth to a boy, the midwife warns her to avoid eating avocado for at least three months. Why? Because if the mother eats avocado before three months have passed the baby's penis will swell, obviously.

Walking back to our hostel, I shook my head in disbelief at their strange customs. I mean, all indigenous cultures have their share of rituals and traditions that modern people find ridiculous – I'm not picking on the Mayans. It's just amazing to me that we, as humans, have advanced from our chicken-waving origins to develop societies that can perform heart transplants, walk on the moon and clone goats.

Goat-cloning aside, I felt a little bit off from the moment we exited the church in San Juan Chamula. I don't know if it was all the smoke, or perhaps the nasty pay toilet I'd used[1], but I had sort of that weak, shivery, achy feeling that precludes a bout of the flu. Of course, since I hadn't actually had the flu in nearly 20 years, I dismissed the feeling as normal travel weariness. Or, I theorized, maybe I was slightly taco-deficient. We found another *colectivo* back to town and I proceeded to remedy the situation with six of the greasiest tacos I'd eaten to date.

That night I was feeling even worse, but again I had an excuse. We had just heard from our family back in the states that we might have to move our stuff into a new storage unit upon our return. I figured the news was actually making me physically sick – moving all that stuff would be a nightmare, and I had vowed that the next time I moved it would be the last.

So, at dinner I decided to play it safe. Iron stomach or not, I ordered plain rice and beans. But then I couldn't help myself. As soon as the meal arrived, I doused the whole thing with hot sauce, ordered a beer and dug into the giant plate of guacamole that Liz had ordered. So much for stomach-friendly.

I still felt achy and weak after dinner, but it wasn't until we went to bed and turned off the lights that things got really nasty. The acid in my stomach was gurgling and boiling away – I could tell that something wasn't right. I tried turning over and lying face down, which usually helps when I have an upset stomach. Wasn't working. Suddenly I remembered that

---

[1] This was the single worst toilet we found anywhere in the world. Yes, it was worse than Calogero and Rosina's. It was worse than the toilet in *Trainspotting*. It was worse than the filthiest squat toilets in Asia. In the interest of not causing you, the reader, to re-enact the projectile vomiting I am about to describe in this chapter, I will leave it at that.

I still possessed a single "Antacil" tablet left over from Thailand. The pills tasted like SweetTarts laced with battery acid and hadn't done much for me in the past, but I was getting desperate. It couldn't hurt to try. Or could it?

Evidently it could. Something in the Antacil seemed to react poorly with the junk already boiling around in my stomach. The pain and nausea intensified. I tossed and turned and groaned and made it impossible for Liz to get any rest. Still, I believed it would pass. Just when I thought it couldn't get any worse, surprisingly, it *did* pass. As long as I stayed in one particular position – halfway between on my side and on my back – I seemed to be OK. I drifted off to sleep.

I don't remember what I was dreaming about. But whatever it was, it vanished in an instant as I woke up and knew with absolute certainty that my magnificent non-vomiting streak was about to come to an end. I remembered exactly what it felt like to be on the verge of throwing up even though I had never experienced the feeling as an adult. The excess saliva, that bitter, salty taste. Wow. I wasn't just going to break the streak, I was going to destroy it in epic fashion.

Tragically, we were in a hostel with a shared bathroom – and it was down the hall. I threw the covers off and bolted out the door, already covering my mouth with my hand. But it had been raining furiously in San Cristobal for the past several days and water had leaked through the skylights and onto the hallway floor. I stopped myself from sprinting just in time to avoid a nasty fall.

Keeping it to a brisk walk, still covering my mouth, I made it to the bathroom, opened the door and turned on the light just in time to witness an amazing

Mexican flag of vomit[1] spew forth from my mouth onto the door, the sink, the floor, the wall and my legs. It went everywhere. Well, everywhere except the toilet bowl.

Oh, our fellow hostel-dwellers were going to love this. I tiptoed the rest of the way to the toilet through my mess and proceeded to violently heave a few more times. When the sickness finally subsided, I stood up and surveyed the damage. I couldn't help but laugh – there I was, coated with and surrounded by my own vomit, wearing nothing but boxers and a T-shirt in a cold, wet, stinky shared hostel bathroom – and I felt absolutely terrific.

It was so cathartic to blast all of that junk out of my stomach, I didn't even mind cleaning up the mess myself, right then and there. Liz woke up and tried to help me, but I waved her off. I'd actually managed to get all the puke inside the bathroom, which made it easy to simply run the shower and hose everything down the drain. A few minutes later I had the whole place looking as good as new, and – teeth brushed and legs washed – I was ready to go back to bed and finally get some decent sleep.

Sadly, sleep was not in the cards that night. The initial euphoria of feeling like the worst was over wore off quickly, and I realized that my stomach wasn't done torturing me yet. The same horrible gurgling started up again, only this time it was worse – psychologically speaking – because I knew that most of the food was gone. Shouldn't I be feeling better?

I tried curling up into a ball, spreading out and lying like a starfish on my stomach – nothing worked. Then I tried to find the magic position I'd used to actually catch a wink of sleep earlier. It wasn't

---

[1] White rice, red flecks of tomato and green from the guacamole. I'm not sure what happened to the beans.

happening. I sweated and cursed and pulled the pillows over my head in despair. Worse, I was starting to feel the effects of dehydration, and, as I began cramping up, I suspected that some of the contaminated food or water must have made its way into my lower digestive system. Oh dear God.

At that moment, lying in a pool of my own sweat, wracked with thirst, I wanted nothing more in the world than an ice-cold soft drink. Please, God, deliver me a huge, sparkling 7-Up filled with shiny ice cubes. Or a deliciously fizzy Coke in a frozen glass bottle. I needed something, *anything,* to settle my stomach and replenish my bodily fluids. I would have happily run out into the street in my boxers to pick something up, but I knew it was hopeless. It was approaching 3am... all the little bodegas would be closed and probably wouldn't re-open until after 8am. I had at least five more miserable hours ahead of me with no salvation in sight. Why, oh why, didn't our hostel have a cooler filled with ice-cold drinks?

Suddenly it hit me. I was praying to the gods for soda. Sweet sassy Jesus, I'd gone indigenous! Or maybe, the people of San Juan Chamula weren't so crazy after all – soda *is* a glorious thing to be worshipped and respected. Didn't I feel like an idiot for belittling their beliefs in my head earlier that day. Now the Soda Gods were punishing me with a furious tornado of vomit and diarrhea the likes of which I'd never experienced before. If I could have had Liz wave a live chicken over my body and rub some eggs on my chest at that point, I may have just given it a shot.

The next morning my prayers were finally answered when Liz ventured forth and brought back a bottle of nice, fizzy Sprite and the best-tasting lemon-lime Gatorade in the history of the universe. Sure, I still wound up sprinting between the toilet and the bed all day long, but my newfound nectar of the gods – soda – made the experience slightly less hellish.

A few days later I was fully recovered, but my non-puking streak was shattered beyond repair. To this day, my dad is still working on something like 35 years without throwing up; there was no way I could ever catch him now. No matter. All it takes is a little creative re-branding to make my streak sound nearly as impressive as it was before the trip. Ahem. I have not thrown up from anything other than drinking *within the continental United States* for the past 21 years.

17. A Love Letter to Portland, Oregon

I'm certainly not the first person to profess his love for Portland, Oregon in print. None other than Chuck Palahniuk – author of *Fight Club* and arguably the most famous Portland-based writer ever – has written an entire book about my quirky hometown. But even though this ground has been well-covered[1], I feel this chapter will help put some of my bitching into perspective. When you love where you live, a lot of the rest of the world is going to seem crappy by comparison.

This brings up, of course, sort of a chicken-and-egg conundrum. Most people have a fondness – or at least some sort of appreciation – for their hometown. Is that all this is? Do I only love Portland so much because I was born here? Would I be writing the same book if I were from Kenosha, Wisconsin instead?

I finally feel I've reached a point in my life where I've seen enough of the United States – and the rest of the world – to definitively say no, there *is* something special about Portland. Plenty of other cities and countries have merit, but none approaches the unique cultural mix and physical location that make Portland so appealing to me.

Growing up, I didn't realize Portland was different. I thought it was normal to have so many trees and parks everywhere. I didn't understand why people from the Midwest or East Coast sometimes made a big deal out of seeing the Pacific Ocean or Mount Hood. And I obviously wasn't old enough to appreciate the

---

[1] It seems the backlash against Portland's popularity has already begun. See "Stuff White People Like" for further examples.

nascent beer-brewing and beer-enjoying culture that was growing up around me.

Truly, I can't say I began to appreciate Portland for what it was until I was nearly thirty years old. Only after living in a variety of cities up and down the West Coast and visiting a decent chunk of the rest of the country – and of course this little trip around the world – did I fully appreciate how special Portland is.

The first time I lived away from Portland was when I was 17, starting my freshman year at the University of Puget Sound in Tacoma, Washington. If you hadn't already guessed based on the Crack House experiences I described in *Hostile Living*, I had a great time at UPS. But this was more *in spite of* than *because of* the fact that the University was located in Tacoma. See, Tacoma just isn't that great of a town, college or otherwise.

A lot of it has to do with the competition. Airlift Tacoma into the middle of South Dakota and suddenly the place looks a lot more appealing. But it's not even in the conversation when you start talking about the best places to live on the West Coast – major cities like Seattle, Portland, San Francisco and Los Angeles simply blow it out of the water, and it even has a hard time holding its own against smaller towns like Bend, Bellingham, Olympia and Eugene[1].

And then there's the "aroma" factor. Anyone who visited Tacoma prior to the late 1990s probably remembers a faint – but distinct – whiff of ass in the air. The scent was largely attributed to a nearby paper mill, but a copper smelting plant unfortunately located

---

[1] For what it's worth, I liken Tacoma to Vancouver, Washington – a second-rate but non-terrible place to live that happens to be located right next to a great place to live. Only Vancouver is closer to Portland than Tacoma is to Seattle, and has a better nickname. Advantage: The Couv.

at the south end of (what could have otherwise been) a magnificent waterfront also contributed to the foul bouquet.

By the time I arrived in 1995 the aroma itself was mostly gone, but the name had stuck. I mean, come on. The Tacoma Aroma? A name that catchy simply doesn't go away overnight. The place could smell like Jessica Alba's underwear drawer and yet the nickname would live on.

In addition to having the reputation of stinking like ass, Tacoma was also at one time one of the most dangerous places to live in America. Again, by the time I arrived some of the worst neighborhoods had been cleaned up, but the downtown area remained sterile and boring at best.

Bad nickname, boring downtown, an inferiority complex from years of playing second-fiddle to Seattle – all of these things obscured the fact that Tacoma actually does have the potential to become a great place to live. There's an amazing neighborhood that looks as if it could have been plucked from the Bay Area just north of the university. The waterfront has been cleaned up and is now a decent place to spend a sunny weekend afternoon. I've heard – though I haven't been back to visit in almost a decade – that the downtown area is even showing signs of life.

So don't get me wrong, I'd rather live in Tacoma than a lot of places on this Earth, but with Seattle less than 40 minutes away, I never figured on spending much time south of Sea-Tac once I graduated. Sure enough, I was bound for the Emerald City by the end of the summer after I graduated.

It was a weird, exciting time to live in Seattle. This was 1999, so everyone was becoming – or had already become – monumentally[1] rich from the dot-

---

[1] And often temporarily.

com explosion. I got my first full-time writing gig at Citysearch.com, a then-young internet company, and naturally expected to become a millionaire within five years. After one performance review, during which a co-worker and I were awarded only small raises but a chance to purchase stock options, I actually told her that, if possible, I would elect to be paid *entirely* in stock options. I still thank my lucky stars that this wasn't allowed to happen.

Regardless of all the dot-com craziness, Seattle is probably my second-favorite city in the world. Like Portland, it's close to both the Pacific Ocean and more snow-capped peaks than you could snowboard in a single season. The summers are glorious, with daylight stretching nearly to 10pm and temperatures in the mid 80s – hot enough for your favorite activities involving water and sunshine, but not so hot and humid that you can't stand being outside for more than 5 minutes. The winters are gray and rainy, it's true, but constant showers keep the air bracingly fresh and clean while intensifying the vibrant colors of the wilderness that surrounds the city.

And, hard as it may be to admit as a Portland native, Seattle is prettier than Portland. Head north on the Alaskan Way Viaduct as the sun is setting for a view that absolutely destroys anything Portland has to offer. To your left the sun dips behind the Cascades, creating a magnificent sunset that reflects off a vast stretch of Elliot Bay. To your right is Seattle's sparkling cityline, capped by the Space Needle at its extreme north end.

Working in Pioneer Square[1] and living in the Fremont neighborhood, I made that drive every workday for two years. When I wasn't working or driving, I was out enjoying the city. I learned about

---

[1] Our office was across the street from the Kingdome. When they blew the thing up, it actually cracked my window.

great food and great music in Seattle, going out to dinner and rock shows with restaurant and music-reviewing friends. For the first time ever, I really got to know a city in-and-out. Even though I'd lived in Portland for 17 years, you could have dropped me on a random street corner and I wouldn't have known which direction we were facing – I had simply never needed to know.

But for all its wonderful attributes, Seattle has a couple major downsides. First and foremost, a house in Seattle proper costs roughly twice as much as an equivalent house in Portland. As a guy with an English degree – someone who decided to make a career in the notoriously tough and generally poorly-compensated field of writing – I began to realize that I may never make enough money to afford a home in the city.

Which would be fine, I guess, if I didn't mind living in the suburbs. But that brings us to Seattle's second crucial flaw: traffic. With over 3.4 million people residing in the city and surrounding metropolitan area, and a highway system designed by a thousand monkeys working with a thousand abacuses and a faxed copy of an MC Escher blueprint[1], Seattle obviously has horrific traffic problems. Mainly, there are about a million people in the suburbs that need to get into the city, about a million people in the city that need to get out to the suburbs, and only one major highway connecting the two.

Still, I loved living in Seattle and would probably have stayed much longer if my career hadn't demanded that I move elsewhere. The dot-com bubble

---

[1] Seattle also has a "Monorail to Nowhere," which runs just over a mile from the Seattle Center (home of the Space Needle) to a downtown mall. It functions as an effective commuter solution for approximately 0.00001% of the city's population.

was already beginning to burst, and it was made clear to me that my future at Citysearch lay at the company's corporate headquarters in Pasadena, California.

Within a few short months I had a new position at Citysearch's main office on Colorado Boulevard in Pasadena, but nowhere to live. The company would only put me up in a hotel for so long, so I had some serious apartment-hunting to do. I wound up settling in a glorified guest-house behind one of Old Pasadena's mansions with a couple of Caltech students. It was more rent than I'd ever paid before and we didn't even have our own laundry facilities, but at least I was in a nice neighborhood and less than a mile from work.

The first year I spent in California, I couldn't get over the nagging sensation that I should be outside all the time. See, in the Pacific Northwest, you don't squander any nice days, because you know the dreary, rainy days aren't far off. In Pasadena, any time I found myself without anything specific to do, perhaps sitting in my apartment idly playing videogames, I felt guilty. *I can't believe I'm wasting this nice day*, I'd think to myself. Then I'd remember that every day was a nice day and go back to *Gran Turismo 3* for another six hours.

In addition to the unbeatable weather, So Cal has a ton of other attributes that Portland and Seattle can't compete with. Sure, the Oregon coast is great, but it ain't Malibu. And the celebrity culture – in which the prospect of not just meeting but actually socializing with pop culture icons during a random night out on the town is a reality – is heady and intoxicating.

When our office moved from Pasadena to downtown Wilshire Boulevard, I ditched my Caltech homeboys and sought out a place at the beach. I was taking on a whole lot more commute, but I figured my proximity to one of the nicest strips of sand in the area – Manhattan Beach – would make up for it.

Long story short, it didn't quite work out that way. I loved the beach, and I had a lot of fun with my new roommates. But the daily two-hour commute was taking its toll. I had lucked my way into kind of a dream job – writing about movies in LA – but the long, hot, horrible drive to and from work every day was crushing my soul. I thought about quitting all the time, but never had the guts to actually go through with it. Finally, in late 2003 the company saved me the trouble and downsized me – in either the fourth or fifth round of layoffs since I had started working at Citysearch in 1999.

By this point, Liz and I were married and living in our own apartment at the beach. We had just moved all our stuff in mere months before, but the opportunity was too good to pass up – we could finally move back to Portland. After an agonizing experience with a Penske rental truck (we broke down near Sacramento and we were forced to unload and reload all our earthly possessions in the middle of the night), we did just that.

From 2004 to 2007, I came to appreciate Portland for more than just being my hometown. It was the first time I'd spent any real time in the city as an adult, and I finally got to know the place intimately. We bought a house in the Mount Tabor area and took constant advantage of its namesake park, built around the remains of an extinct volcano. We walked over to the developing Montavilla neighborhood for coffee or a flick at our shiny new second-run movie house, where the tickets were $3 each and you could drink beer and eat pizza throughout the show. Liz joined hordes of bicycle commuters as she pedaled across town to Portland State University, where she was enrolled in a graduate program. And I rode my motorcycle a wonderfully short 4 miles to work each day, rain or shine.

These are all nice things, and good attributes for a city to have. But none is unique to Portland – lots of cities have great parks, cool coffeehouses and bike lanes. The thing is, Portland is more than the sum of its parts. I mean, yes, it's an ideally-sized city in a great location between the mountains and the beach with lots of breweries and strip clubs and probably the best bookstore in the world, but what makes the town extra-special to me is that you could be walking around the Clinton neighborhood and run into a mob of drunken Santas. On a Tuesday. In July.

I always thought I was kind of a weird kid growing up, but by Portland's standards I was almost frighteningly normal. It's like my whole generation reached a point (sometime around 1996 by my estimation) where they collectively decided that they didn't give a fuck about what anyone thought – they were going to put on some eyeliner and zebra tights and ride their unicycles around Pioneer Square at lunch. While I don't personally care to partake in this activity, I love that I *could*, and I'd still only be like the third-weirdest person in a one-block radius.

Yes, this is a city where one might, if one were so inclined, attach a disfigured clown doll to the rear bumper of his or her car using a rope noose and casually run errands without drawing too many looks. It's a city where the Church of Elvis (now only available online) gets more attention than the Catholic Church. We pioneered the Robitussin flavored donut[1], invented Claymation[2], re-popularized the brakeless, fixed-gear

---

[1] Formerly available at Voodoo Donuts until the buzzkills at the FDA complained about this innovative combination of pharmaceutical and foodstuff. Sadly, "take two donuts and call me in the morning" is no longer a valid prescription.
[2] Remember those California Raisins commercials? Yeah, that was Portland.

bicycle[1] and are the proud owners of one of the world's finest velvet art museums.

But we're not just weird for the sake of weird. And we're not all weird. Portland is sophisticated enough to have a thriving culinary scene. Cultured enough to support a diverse theater scene. Drunken enough to boast more breweries per capita than *any other city in the world*. Take that, Milwaukie and every city in Germany.

Long story short, as I lay dying in a stinky Mexican hostel, vomiting and shitting and crying, all I could think about was how much better I had it back home. I mean, I found the best place in the world to live... why did I ever leave? And for this? We still had months to go in Mexico, and things would get better. We'd find great food, meet new friends and have many more adventures. But was it really worth the price we were paying? All the sickness we'd endure, missing birthdays and holidays and all the comforts of home?

---

[1] Okay, this is actually a mark against Portland.

18. Okay, Fine, It Was All Worth It.

I believe Happy Gilmore said it best. *I'm stupid, you're smart. I was wrong, you were right. You're the best, I'm the worst. You're very good looking, I'm not very attractive.* Still, admitting that I had a good time on our trip didn't prevent me from being insanely excited to return home at the end. I've been trying to think of a pithy word or phrase to describe the feeling I experienced upon finally arriving back in Portland, Oregon. Something that means almost exactly the opposite of "culture shock." Culture enjoyment? Culture appreciation? Culture complacency?

Maybe the word I'm thinking of is relief. Culture relief. We actually did it – traveled all the way around the world and then some, braving turbulent flights, legitimately dangerous bus rides, bugs, sketchy foods, open sewers, aggressive restaurant touts and more – and managed to touch down in Portland without our last flight crashing semi-ironically into the Pacific Ocean[1].

Yep, despite everyone assuring us we would be bamboozled by the sights and sounds of our native country after such a long time away from the United States, we didn't experience much culture shock at all. I didn't walk into my favorite grocery store and fall to my knees in ecstasy like I thought I might. Nor did I drive straight to a fast-food restaurant and gorge myself on cheeseburgers.

In fact, after a few days it hardly felt like we had been gone at all. It was actually kind of disappointing. I

---

[1] As a writer, the idea of experiencing a trite, ironic death (you know, ten thousand spoons when all you need is a knife) really bothers me.

mean, it was great to see our family and friends again, don't get me wrong. But the reality of having to put our lives back together soon overshadowed our enjoyment of all the things we'd been missing.

No matter how hard you try to think of everything, there's just no way to plan for a 10-month absence from the USA. Things expire. Stuff gets lost. Even the people you should be able to count on to be responsible for the things you've left behind – your parents – could "misplace" your keys[1]. We came back to to America with open arms and smiles on our faces, rushing to embrace her clean standards of living and efficient everyday life. But instead, America bitch-slapped us like we were common guests on Jerry Springer.

The first nasty surprise was that our driver's licenses had been suspended. Following the advice of our insurance agent, we didn't cancel our coverage before leaving, but we did lower it to a "storage" level while our car was gathering paw-prints and mice in the engine as it sat inactive at the family farm in Washington. But when the ever-vigilant Oregon DMV did a random check and found that we weren't carrying liability insurance, they went right ahead and suspended our licenses. The system works!

Upon our return to the Land of the Free, we didn't have jobs, insurance, incomes, cell phones or a permanent address. Our taxes were overdue, our gym memberships were frozen and we had a box of mail waiting for us that would give your average carrier a hernia. Liz had a medical bill that somehow slipped through the cracks go to collection while we were gone, and when she tried to call and explain that it should have been covered by our previous insurance carrier,

---

[1] Still waiting on these, guys.

the billing department crossed their wires and put through *another* $100 charge on the account.

And I haven't even gotten started on the storage situation. I wanted to play basketball but my shoes were buried in storage. We wanted catastrophic health insurance but our marriage certificate was buried in storage[1]. Liz wanted to ride her bicycle to the grocery store, but her panniers were buried in storage. I wanted to do SOMETHING, ANYTHING, but my ENTIRE FUCKING LIFE WAS BURIED IN STORAGE. Worse, we tried to save money by storing our stuff in a family member's basement, only to be forced to MOVE EVERYTHING WE OWNED TWO MORE TIMES BEFORE EVEN GETTING TO USE ANY OF IT!

Excuse me. It's just that it was a very close call between moving our 2,000 cubic feet of storage an extra two times and simply lighting myself on fire to avoid the hassle.

Of course, all these inconveniences were wildly annoying, but the real kicker came when I opened a letter from Wells Fargo and found a check for over $2,300 in my name[2]. Wow, just when I was starting to worry about the amount of money we were spending before either of us had a job, this windfall completely put my mind at ease. Hey, this check could pay for a third of a motorcycle! Without rent to worry about, this check could cover our expenses for months! Hey, wait a sec... this check... this check is expired. Son of a god damn bitch.

You know, one of the things that annoyed me most about the third world countries we visited was the

---

[1] My wife kept her last name when we got married – a decision that has now officially cost us $7.75 in backup copies of our marriage certificate at the county office.
[2] Payout from the escrow account on our home mortgage, something we hadn't even considered before leaving the country.

lack of order and regulation. People can drive their cars and motorbikes wherever and however they like. You don't need permits to build things. Chaos reigns supreme.

I couldn't wait to get back to the States, where things just seemed to make sense. But what I failed to realize was that the tradeoff is red tape. We're clean and organized, that much is true. But we have to deal with insurance forms and licenses and proof of residency and expiration dates in exchange. Isn't it kind of... I dunno... simpler without all that crap?

Okay, hang on a second. I feel nauseous. I think it's because I actually learned something from all this traveling, which officially makes this a "book where a WASPY dude travels, learns something about himself and then writes it down." In fact, this whole chapter is damn close to a rumination. I need to run and stick my finger down my throat, brb.

All right, I'm better now. Just realizing that I could walk across the street and choose from 20 different brightly-colored antacids is helping. I reserve the right to chug Pepto-Bismol at any point in this chapter as I continue ruminating on the lessons we can learn from our friends in the third world.

Of course, it's more than just the red tape that's bugging me. The real truth is that the grass is always greener. Coming back to the USA wasn't as amazing as I hoped it would be because nothing could live up to my expectations. This is how travel, and life, works: You dream about something and work hard to achieve it, only to find it's not as great as you were hoping it would be. Afterward, when it's gone, you forget all the negatives and wish you still had it.

If I die and am reincarnated as a cow, I am going to laugh my ass off at the other cows that are trying to get to those greener pastures on the other side of the hill, secure in my knowledge that the grass on my side is just as good. Actually, that's not true. I think I've always known that the figurative grass in life always seems greener elsewhere (when it frequently isn't), but that doesn't mean I can stop myself from pining after that super-awesome ultra-green grass I occasionally glimpse.

And now, in a lengthy, heartwarming paragraph that will serve as my best hope of getting into Oprah's book club and consequently raking in millions of dollars, I will say that the only thing we can do about this condition – the human condition – is to take time each and every day to appreciate what we've got. There were times when I found myself sitting on a dazzling white beach in Thailand, dipping my toes into the cool, refreshing water and dreaming of cold, wet, gray, rainy old Portland. What the fuck? How could I not appreciate the literal paradise I was sitting in at that moment? Never mind why I'm wired this way; I just am. I think most people are, and there's probably nothing we can do about it. But it really does help me to enjoy life more when I take a few seconds to reflect on how incredibly fortunate I am at least once a day. Hey, look at me, I'm sitting on the beach, drinking a beer that only cost a dollar, and I haven't worked in over 200 days. Life is pretty fucking good.

I think I said "fuck" a little too much for Oprah's tastes, but fuck it, I'm leaving it in.

19. Paradise Found

Now that we've nearly reached the end of the book, and everything is out in the open (spoiler alert if you're skipping around: *The Reluctant Traveler* had a good time on his 10-month trip around the world, bet you never saw that coming), I guess I can go ahead and rant and rave about some of my favorite places in the world like an average, non-Reluctant travel writer might.

Indeed, there were some spots we visited on our trip that even I couldn't find flaw with. Places that, against all odds, were actually *better* than any gushing Conde Nast copy could possibly describe. That's right, these are the kind of places that can turn even the most jaded, hardened travel writer into an adjective-spewing newbie. From well-known spots that have become underrated over the years, to the dreaded "hidden gems off the beaten path," these are the places that made our trip – 400 hours of horrible bus rides included – totally worth it. Without further ado, I give you Paradise Found.

Buenos Aires, Argentina

BsAs is one of the 15 largest cities in the world – comparable in size to New York, London, Tokyo or Paris – but you never hear it mentioned in the same breath as those cities. Bad for Buenos Aires and its still-recovering economy, I suppose, but good for you as a traveler.

The city is every bit as fashionable as Paris, hip as London, awe-inspiring as New York and about a million times cheaper than Tokyo. The fact that it's approximately 82,000 miles away from everything else is probably the only thing keeping it off most travelers' radar screens.

You'll find great, European-inspired cuisine, remarkable wine, the best ice cream in the world[1] and of course, that tender, juicy Argentinean beef – all for a fraction of the cost relative to anywhere else. Seriously, how much would a fancy dinner for two and a bottle of wine cost in New York? $250? $300? Spend that much in Buenos Aires and you'll get two bottles of the best wine on the menu and roughly 200 ounces of steak. Better ask for a doggie bag.

It's an easy city to explore. A bus ride across town costs about 30 cents. Or you can ride in style in a private cab for just a few dollars more – fare from one side of the city to the other shouldn't run you more than $6 or $7. And while the half-European, half-modern cityscape is well worth checking out, Buenos Aires isn't just a concrete jungle; the city has some of the best urban green spaces this side of Central Park.

Even something you might normally consider mundane – the sidewalks – are grand in Buenos Aires. Thanks to a tradition of public officials misappropriating government funds for their own glory, the city has undertaken all manner of opulent public works projects throughout its history, resulting in massive open-air plazas, 15-lane roads flanked by sidewalks as wide as Interstate-5, fountains, statues, pillars, roundabouts and government palaces. It's an urban planner's wet dream.

And as an added bonus for other pale, white Reluctant Travelers out there, you won't stick out like a sore thumb in Buenos Aires. It's a welcome change of

---

[1] Yes, even better than the gelato in Italy. We confirmed this unusual finding over and over again with a thoroughly scientific series of samplings.

pace from the Unbearable Whiteness of Being you might experience in Asia, where Caucasian westerners like me can't make it more than a block or two without someone trying to sell us something.

The only thing approaching a downside is the city's reputation for arrogance and rudeness – and we found it to be highly overrated. In fact, the only problem you will likely have in Buenos Aires is finding a way to spend your vast financial holdings – big bills are hard to break because many shopkeeps are loath to part with their precious peso coins.

So go already, if you want to experience one of the greatest cities in the world at a bargain basement price. It's only going to get more expensive – the "Paris of South America" was once just as costly to visit as the real Paris, and I'm betting it will be once again.

El Calafate, Argentina – Perito Moreno Glacier

While you're in Argentina, it would be a crime to miss nothing less than the most breathtaking natural phenomenon I've ever witnessed. I'll admit that, on paper, glaciers don't sound very exciting. They generally don't move, explode or light up at night. And it's not like I've never seen one before. We have glaciers in the Pacific Northwest – right up on Mount Hood, in fact. And while Mount Hood is scenic and spectacular in its own right, the glaciers blend into rest of the landscape so you would never even notice them. I'm fairly certain I have stood on one or more of Mount Hood's glaciers without even realizing it.

Argentina's glaciers are different, especially Perito Moreno. While not a particularly large glacier in the grand scheme of things, it's notable precisely for the way in which it sticks out from the surrounding landscape – just a huge, impossibly blue wall of ice that extends as far as the eye can see – wedged in between a couple of hills. And unlike your boring, stereotypical mountain glacier, this sucker is active.

What that means is that every couple of minutes, absurdly large chunks of ice "calve" off of the face of the glacier with a tremendous booming crack and fall into the water below, creating a massive wave. I guess with global warming and all this sort of glacier behavior is probably fairly common in Antarctica or the North Pole, but the reality is that most of us will never see either of those places except on the Discovery Channel. In El Calafate, Argentina, you can stare this raw expression of nature in the face until you go snow blind or your tour bus abandons you, whichever comes first.

Or, you can actually hike on the glacier itself. We didn't, unfortunately, and it's one of my only real regrets about our trip. It's expensive to book the glacier-walking tour, and at the time I simply couldn't imagine that it would be worth it. After all, I'd stood on glaciers on Mount Hood! Call me an irresponsible journalist, but I'm going to go ahead and recommend that you pay whatever they're asking to walk on the glacier – even though I haven't done it myself. Then, go and book the other tour too – the basic "catwalk" tour that we did – just to see the thing from another angle. It really is that good.

I must now offer two caveats to my recommendation, but neither one should stop you from seeing Perito Moreno. The first is that El Calafate – the town closest to the glacier – is nothing special by Patagonia's standards. Sure, it's scenic and nicely developed, and it offers access to nearby alpine sports. But the glacier is really the only reason to go there. If you're looking for some kind of rustic town where you can hardly turn around without running into a majestic Andean peak, check out El Chalten instead[1].

The second caveat is that El Calafate is about as far away as you can get from everything else in the world without actually leaving the planet. Take a look at a globe the next time you get a chance – El Calafate is waaaaay down there. Think about how long it would take you to get to Buenos Aires from the states, then realize that you've got another *two* 25-hour bus rides just to get to Rio Gallegos. Complete all that and you've only got one more six hour bus ride to go! Not counting the two-hour ride from El Calafate to the Perito Moreno glacier itself, of course. Really, it is worth the effort. But if you have the means, consider flying.

Sukhothai, Thailand

Right off the bat, let me just state for the record that I'm not much of a ruin guy. I mean, sure, I enjoy seeing ancient buildings and statues, but the more "ruined" they are, the less I typically enjoy them. I like my statues with the arms and heads still attached. I prefer the Pantheon to the Parthenon. And I'll choose St. Peter's cathedral over the Coliseum every day of the week and twice on Sunday. But that doesn't mean there aren't any ruins I'm interested in seeing.

There's Machu Picchu. The Great Wall. Egypt's pyramids. And of course, Angkor Wat, which Liz and I actually did visit while we were in Asia. While all these

---

[1] If Liz had written this chapter, El Chalten would be at the top of her list. Google it – it's pretty incredible. But El Calafate gets the nod in my book, simply because you can see awe-inspiring mountains just about anywhere, but the Perito Moreno glacier is unique.

ancient attractions are, to some degree, ruined, they're still impressive enough to warrant a visit at some point in my lifetime. The only problem? They're simply too popular for their own good.

Sad as it may be to admit, I've become a travel snob. I have a hard time appreciating the grandeur and significance of a two thousand year-old temple when I'm being elbowed and nudged from every side by a group of 65 Japanese tourists. Plus, it's hard to clear your mind and imagine the world as it existed when these structures were brand new when you see the flash and hear the digital whirr of a camera every 1.5 seconds. So yeah, Angkor Wat was cool, and I'd see it again, but I didn't leave inspired. I left regretting that I hadn't seen the thing before it was completely overrun.

Here's the Catch-22. There's a place we visited on our trip that was almost as amazing as Angkor Wat. It was practically free[1] and virtually deserted. But by mentioning it in this book, I'm helping to destroy the very qualities that made the site so interesting to me. How can I do that? Isn't it hypocritical to complain that some of the best tourist attractions in the world are ruined by masses of tourists, then turn around and promote an "unknown" attraction, thereby ruining it? How can I live with myself?

Turns out I can live with myself just fine. Look, I can't worry about whether I'm helping ruin some of my favorite places in the world by writing about them. That's an issue for the local communities to deal with. I hear that whoever's in charge of Machu Picchu has begun severely restricting the number of entrants

---

[1] Admission was less than $5 per person and you could rent a bicycle to explore the entire site for about $0.75 per day. By comparison, Angkor Wat runs close to $25 per person, and the tuk-tuk mafia will berate you into paying a boatload for a chauffeured ride.

allowed into the park each day. That's great news – it'll
make the experience so much better for the ones that
get in. Everyone else can wait their turn and be
rewarded with a more fulfilling visit for their patience.

So, Sukhothai, Thailand. The cat's out of the
bag. The funny thing is that the bag's been untied this
whole time – I'm not sure why the cat didn't escape
earlier. See, Thailand itself is a little too popular for its
own good. For every spot that remains pristine and
undeveloped, there's another that has its own
McDonald's and Starbucks. So it's kind of surprising to
me that we'd find such a magnificent architectural
wonder being almost completely ignored just a few
hours north of Bangkok.

I'll say it again: Objectively, Sukhothai is *not* as
in-your-face impressive as Angkor Wat. But for every
fifty tourists that visit Angkor Wat, perhaps one will
visit Sukhothai. That means you'll actually be able to
stand and appreciate the crumbling statues without
jockeying for position with forty other people. You can
pedal a flimsy Chinese bicycle around the entire site in
peace, free from the incessant traffic whine of
motorbikes and tuk-tuks. And, best of all, we didn't
find a single trinket or souvenir available for sale
within a hundred yards of any park entrance.

Except for their respective levels of popularity,
Angkor Wat and Sukhothai are remarkably similar.
Just as Angkor Wat was the capital city of an ancient
Cambodian kingdom, Sukhothai was the first Thai
capital. Both sites are massive grids made up of
temples, statues, ruined structures and man-made
pools of water. Off the top of my head I'd estimate that
Angkor Wat is larger, but the site at Sukhothai will still
take you hours to explore on bicycle. It doesn't have as
many individual attractions as Angkor Wat, but the
wide-open layout and relatively sparse placement of

ruins are a big part of what make Sukhothai so charming.

First off, the grounds are beautiful. There are lots of trees and shade, and the site's northerly location makes for cooler temperatures than at Angkor Wat[1]. And the water is everywhere, which means you get great reflections of the many wats[2] and the lush vegetation surrounding them. Plus, the statues and temples themselves are nothing to sneeze at. You'll find 40 and 50 foot tall Buddhas that are still mostly intact, the aforementioned wats – great bell shapes that culminate in impossibly skinny skyward pinnacles – and more ruined structures than you can shake a stick at.

You can take in the entirety of Sukhothai's attractions in two days. On the first day, sleep in late, have a banana pancake and a mixed fruit shake at one of the nearby cafés for breakfast, then rent yourself a Chinese bicycle for two days. Bring water, sunscreen and a camera – and just spend the day leisurely pedaling around the park, stopping when and where you want. Don't worry if you miss something; that's what the second day is for.

Now, if you want to have kind of a freaky, unique experience, here's a recommendation we picked up from the owner of the Orchid Hibiscus guest house[3]. Get to bed early the first night so you can wake up before the break of dawn the next day. Pedal your ass down to the park – to "Wat Si Chum," specifically – before the sun rises. You won't necessarily get a great sunrise from that vantage point, but the experience of

---

[1] The day we visited Angkor Wat, it was roughly the same temperature outside as it was on the surface of the sun.

[2] The word "wat" pretty much means the same thing in both Cambodia and Thailand – "temple."

[3] The best guest house in Asia. Obviously soon to be overrun by my readers, so get there while you can.

pedaling through a park filled with creepy 40-foot statues in the dark is one I'll never forget.

You should arrive at Wat Si Chum just as dawn is breaking. You will hear some bizarre noises – animal noises. What animal is making that noise? Walk slowly toward the main temple between two rows of ruined pillars. You will see a giant seated Buddha statue peeking out from a small chamber at the very back of the temple. Its eyes are closed in peaceful meditation. You walk closer. The noises are getting louder. It sounds like a chicken eating a dog. That's not possible, is it? Maybe it's a flock of pigeons attacking a single dog. Is someone here? Look around just to make sure. No. You're alone. Walk closer. It really sounds like someone is here. The closer you get to the Buddha, the louder the noises seem to be getting. What in God's name is that noise? You stop in your tracks. You look up at the Buddha again. OH MY GOD ITS EYES ARE OPEN! IT'S STARING RIGHT AT ME! LET'S GET THE FUCK OUT OF HERE!

It's pretty cool.

Bangkok, Thailand

If you're going to visit Southeast Asia, chances are you'll make at least one stop in Bangkok. It's got the biggest and best airport in the region, making it a hub not only for Thailand, but also Laos, Vietnam, Cambodia and even Indonesia. But no matter what your "real" destination is, it's well worth your time to schedule a few extra days to spend in Bangkok itself.

Now, I don't know about you, but before I visited the city, I pictured it as a weird shamble of floating markets and rickshaws. Well, there is at least one notable floating market, but it turns out my uninformed impression was only half right. In addition to being a "sprawling Asian shithole," as Chuck Thompson lovingly refers to it, Bangkok is an honest-to-Jesus modern city, with skyscrapers, billboards, freeways, a subway *and* an elevated train.

I like to think of it as the Las Vegas of Southeast Asia, minus the gambling (well, minus the *legal* gambling), plus about ten times as much sex. It really is the most appropriately-named city in the world. Sex tourism aside, Bangkok simply has this hot-shit, authentic, hard-boiled vibe that makes *you* feel cool just for walking around on its streets. You might be a teetotaling, church-going father of five, but try slinking around Sukhumwit road and you'll feel as if you're up to something exciting and no good, even if you're only there to purchase a counterfeit Rolex.

And just like the other big city I'm recommending in this chapter – Buenos Aires – Bangkok's charms are enhanced by the fact that visiting Americans are relative millionaires. You could drop some serious coin in a slick restaurant with waiters who speak English better than you, or you could get food that's often just as good on the street for literally pennies. I recommend doing both.

Don't get caught up trying to visit every temple in the city. There are too many and they're mostly the same. Instead, spend your time seeking out the best street food, checking out live music and hobnobbing with young Thai hipsters in a variety of late-night hot spots. Do check out the mad market down at Khao San road and the surrounding area, but for the love of God don't rent a room there, unless you are trying to punish yourself for some transgression in a past life.

Various Beaches, Assorted Countries

I've covered a lot of the beaches we visited already, so I'll keep this short and sweet. Here are the best tropical beaches we've visited in the world: Ko Phi Phi Leh ("The Beach," Thailand), Haad Yao (on Ko Pha Ngan, Thailand), Ko Lanta (Thailand), Bamboo Island (near Sihanoukville, Cambodia), Isla Mujeres (Mexico), Tulum (Mexico) and Playa Rincon (Dominican Republic). Told you that would be short.

20. Questions and Answers

As I mentioned at the start of the book, I wrote a lot of this while traveling. Which is obviously lame and super clichéd, but I actually didn't start until we were more than seven months into our trip, and I honestly had nothing better to do on a 22 hour bus ride in northern Argentina. In any case, thinking and writing about traveling while you're actually doing it are pretty different than when you have a couple months of perspective. For example, if you had caught me just as I was stepping on a plane to leave Southeast Asia and asked me whether I'd consider coming back, I would have said *maybe*. Now, less than half a year later, I would jump at an opportunity to visit those countries again.

The point I'm trying to make is that, having been home for a while now, I've finally had time to digest the whole experience. Even when people ask me vague questions, such as the dreaded "How was your trip?" I can give them a well thought-out answer rather than just shrugging and saying *pretty good*.

I will now give you, the reader, the opportunity to pose your own questions in this space, and I will do my best to answer them. Don't worry, you don't need an internet connection for this. I have anticipated all your questions and thoughtfully typed them out for you[1].

---

[1] If on the off-chance I have missed a question you would like to have answered, just visit vivarobusto.com and post it there. I check the site all the time and will do my best to reply. Yes, you will need an internet connection for this.

Q: What kind of a jackass are you? You say you hate traveling and travel writing, and then you travel and write a book about it. Jackass.

A: I really have no counter-argument. Well played. I will point out that I never said that I hate *all* travel writing, or *all* travel. I just hate smarmy, holier-than-thou travel writing, and smarmy, holier-than-thou travel.

Q: All right, fair enough. So how much did the whole trip cost?

A: Ah, I get this question all the time. We spent $40,000 over the course of 10 months. $6,000 went toward our plane tickets, most of the rest covered beer.

Q: What was your favorite country?

A: Another common question, but a really tricky one to answer. I can give you a definite top three, but from there it gets dicey. Here goes: The three best countries we visited were Italy, Thailand and Argentina. I really thought Mexico would be up there but the food wasn't as good as I hoped it would be. The worst country we visited was Qatar. But we only saw the airport so that's not entirely fair.

Q: What was the best meal you had?

A: This one's easy. The best meal we had was in a small town near Parma, Italy, and was prepared by Liz's mother's friend Gail and her husband Gianni. They live in a converted castle and have their own vintner, so it's fair to say they know how to live the good life.

    We started with warm focaccia, sparkling white wine, roughly crumbled Parmigiano and the best salami I have ever tasted. For the main course, Gail served mushroom risotto and a caprese salad along with bottle after bottle of their own red wine, hand-crafted by their personal vintner. And we followed that with a cheese plate, pears, grappa and champagne. Gail, Gianni, if you're reading this, I won't ever be able to treat you guys to such an amazing meal, but I'd love to give it a shot.

Q: What was the worst place you stayed and how much did it cost?
A: Our first room in Vientiane, Laos was pretty bad. It was a windowless concrete barrack with wallpapered floors and no sink. The toilet also lacked a flush handle. It cost $6 and we only stayed one night before breaking down and upgrading to an $18 room. There was also an otherwise stately room in Hoi An, Vietnam that cost only $8 but included a tarantula the size of a baseball.

Q: What was the cheapest place you stayed?
A: We paid $3 a night for a room in Vang Vieng, Laos for nearly a week.

Q: What was the most expensive place you stayed?
A: Mexico *seemed* the most expensive by the time we arrived there, but in reality we spent the most in Italy. I think our room in Vernazza was about $75 for one night.

Q: What was the closest you came to death?
A: I hate to even think about it, but the cab ride in Tucuman I described in Chapter 2 and every time we boarded a bus in Vietnam.

Q: Were you pickpocketed/robbed/assaulted or otherwise molested during your travels?
A: Actually, no. I set down a rain jacket in Hoi An for a minute too long and it disappeared, but that was the extent of our losses. I was pretty vigilant about keeping everything safe, but even I was surprised that we managed to travel for so long without losing anything. We were hustled by countless tuk-tuk drivers, however.

Q: How did you and your wife stay married throughout this ordeal?
A: Ha. Even though we probably seem like radically different people based on the stories I've told in this book, we had a blast together. We're not *Dharma and Greg*.

Q: So you just up and did it, huh? How did you make it happen?
A: I get this one a lot. It seems there are a lot of people out there who have been passively planning a trip like this but haven't yet managed to put it all together. The answer is simple: Save money. Sure, I had poker as a nice second income, but it's not like my first income was so huge to begin with.

Q: But what about your job?
A: Yeah, that's the trickier part. The timing was great for Liz because she had just finished graduate school. Me, I up and quit a perfectly good job, which is something most reasonable people avoid doing. Still, even though I had a good job, I felt as though I needed a sabbatical. I will say that it was a bit of a rude surprise to return to the United States during the

biggest economic meltdown since the Great
Depression.

Q: When are you going to end the book?
A: Right now.

Thank You

The biggest and best thank you obviously goes to my wife Liz, who was both the driving force behind our trip and the whip-cracking motivation that led to me finishing and ultimately publishing this book. She's also been a remarkably good sport about being occasionally made fun of in print. Big thanks to both of our families for supporting us throughout our adventures and spamming friends and strangers alike with our blog while we traveled. Thank you to the internet entity known as Limesparks and/or Limesporks for original cover inspiration. Thank you to Mark Schwander for following through with the complete cover design. Thank you to Bonnie Fazio (my mom), Jeff Martin, Tam Brine, Seth English-Young, Jay Martin, Adam Hersh and Patrick McMahon for reading early manuscripts and offering sage advice. I also have a contractual obligation to thank Peter Heyneman, to whom I promised a book mention in exchange for one tenth of one percent of his 2008 World Series of Poker winnings (which unfortunately amounted to $0.00). Last but not least, thank you to all of the bad poker players across the world that made our trip possible.

10339925R00112

Made in the USA
Charleston, SC
27 November 2011